HOLY
Hiking Boots

Praise for Holy Hiking Boots

Holy Hiking Boots doubles as a daily devotional and an intentional Bible Study all in one. Each story brings with it thoughts for personal application, and the richness of the biblical text makes a girl want to explore the Word deeper and further. My friend and associate Rebecca has done it again. She communicates on such a personal level, and at the same time biblically sound truths are searched out and shouted from the roof tops. You won't regret investing time in this book!
> —PAM BREWER, *Women's Ministry Director,*
> *First Baptist Dallas, Texas*

I have literally watched Rebecca write this book! Each story represents a hearty understanding of God's radical and undeserved grace for broken and messed up people like US! This book is filled with hope and good news. Leave the "How to be a better Christian" books on the shelf and soak in the sweet Gospel that transforms lives. Every page is a gift to you and me."
> —JEFF TAYLOR, *Morning Show Co-Host*
> *"Mornings with Jeff & Rebecca," 90.9 KCBI, Dallas/Fort Worth*

In *Holy Hiking Boots*, Rebecca Carrell invites us into her everyday encounters with God. Moment by moment, she reveals Jesus as her best friend and encourages others to embrace Him in the same way. She paints pictures with stories that reflect her deep passion and experience with the Word of God. This book is for everyone who longs to know Christ in a more intimate and beautiful way. Grab this book and your Bible and step into the adventure of a lifetime.
> —JAN GREENWOOD, *Equip Pastor*
> *Gateway Church, Southlake, Texas*

From the moment I began reading, "Holy Jellybeans," I was inspired by Rebecca's ability to communicate the heart of God through everyday living. Now, through "Holy Hiking Boots," I am inspired by her ability to communicate scripture with such understanding and passion - such a gift! Her realness and honesty draw you in giving you the desire to dig deeper. You will truly be encouraged as you read how God can…. and does make the ordinary extraordinary!
> —SUZIE PRIZOR, *Women's Ministry Director*
> *Parkhills Baptist Church, Plano, TX*

Rebecca has a rare ability to see God working in the everyday things of life. When most of us see routine, Rebecca notices little things that God plans to use for a big message because she lives expectantly. But, she's also in tune with God's loving kindness through heartache, difficult changes, and the unexpected blows that we don't see coming. You'll see yourself in many pages of this book, and find hope and joy for not just in the day to day, but also for the hardest days. Rebecca's goal is not to help you cope. She'll instead point you to the Author and Finisher of our faith in your time of need, whether big or small.

> —MATT AUSTIN, *General Station Manager*
> *90.9 KCBI Dallas/Fort Worth*
> *Kcbi.org*

This is a remarkable book of love, humor, wisdom, courage and integrity. This candid journey of Rebecca's life reveals how Gods hand touches everything our lives.

> —MISTY DANIELS, *Publisher* Living *Magazine*
> *Arlington, Texas*

I love how Rebecca can take the normal things we go through in life, weave a fantastic, visual story and then completely tie it all to the Bible and God's love for us. The way she makes sure we are grounded in His word is not onl y inspiring personally but also gives me so many little Bible nuggets to pass along to the ladies I get to lead in ministry. I'm looking forward to the impact *Holy Hiking Boots* has on Northview's ministry and beyond.

> —ANDREA GIBSON, *Director of Women's Ministry*
> *Northview Baptist Church, Lewisville, TX*

You will greatly benefit from the gift the Lord has given Rebecca Carrell to weave Biblical principles around real life issues. With raw emotion, interesting insights and clear focus she will help you reframe your circumstances around the providence of God in your life's journey. So climb a little higher in your walk with the Lord through "Holy Hiking Boots!"

> —DEBBIE STUART, *Life Coach and Director of Ministry Initiatives*
> *Hope for the Heart, Plano, TX*
> *Serving in Women's Ministry for over 25 years*

When God Makes the Ordinary Extraordinary

Rebecca Ashbrook Carrell

Carpenter's Son Publishing

Holy Hiking Boots
When God Makes the Ordinary Extraordinary

© 2017 by Rebecca Carrell

Published by Carpenter's Son Publishing, Franklin, Tennessee

Published in association with Larry Carpenter
of Christian Book Services, LLC
www.christianbookservices.com

Cover Design by Brett Dougall

Interior Layout by Suzanne Lawing

ISBN: 978-1-946889-03-4

Printed in the United States of America

ACKNOWLEDGMENTS

To Mike Carrell, the best husband on planet earth. Thank you for your tireless support and encouragement. Thank you for loving me through my crazy and talking me off the ledge. None of this would be possible without you. I love you so much.

To Caitlyn and Nick, the coolest kids ever. You have taught me much about the love, grace, mercy, and patience of our Lord. I pray that I exhibit those qualities with you. You are loved more than you can fathom.

Mom and Dad, you never stopped waiting for your prodigal daughter to come home. Thank you for your steadfast love.

To Jeff Taylor, Matt Austin, Joel Burke, and Sharon Geiger. You have given me a voice and a place to cast my visions and chase my dreams. I love serving side by side with you at 90.9 KCBI. Thank you for trusting me and encouraging me to grow.

FOREWORD

Rebecca Ashbrook Carrell is a gifted communicator which you'll discover for yourself within the pages of *Holy Hiking Boots*. With refreshing poise, confidence, humor, instruction, vulnerability, and spiritual sensitivity, Rebecca has a special way of letting you see inside her journey long enough to suddenly find Jesus speaking into yours. Her words have a compelling way of giving dignity to your life, and to mine, in such relatable ways. Rebecca is a captivating storyteller and understands the value of stories in ministry. Jesus used the art of the parable often when talking to others because stories move hearts and hearts touched and transformed by Jesus can move mountains. As you read *Holy Hiking Boots*, I believe Jesus will begin to show you how your story matters and how you are gloriously found within His.

In Rebecca's second book, the sequel to *Holy Jellybeans* you'll discover the same bite-sized nuggets of nourishment, incredibly helpful and easy to incorporate in the busyness of day-to-day life. However, don't mistake the brevity for lack of solid content. These are not snacks; these are full meals packed with power, principle, and meaning.

I also love the fact that *Holy Hiking Boots* is infused with Scripture. Sandwiched between almost every paragraph is God's Word, which shows Rebecca's complete fidelity to the source of everything—the Word of God. Stories are great, but stories grounded in Scripture transform lives.

Holy Hiking Boots reminds us that God can speak to us anytime, through anything. Be prepared to read some wonderful insights that will shape the way you approach life and difficulties.

I love this woman of God, and I love what pours forth from her. Give it a few pages and you will too.

—Carlene "CeCe" Prince
Associate Network Manager, YNOP Radio
Author, Speaker, Singer/Song-writer, Recording
Artist of Carlene Prince Ministries

CONTENTS

INTRODUCTION

Thomas said to Him, "Lord, we do not know where You are going, how do we know the way?" Jesus said to him, "I am the way, and the truth, and the life; no one comes to the Father but through Me."

—John 14:5–6 NASB

I have often wondered what life must have been like for the disciples and followers of Christ during His time on earth.

How did they feel at the end of a long day spent walking and ministering, healing and feeding? Full of hope? Struck mute with awe? Or did the miracles of the master somehow become ordinary, everyday, and expected?

In an article posted on the *Huffington Post* in 2014, blogger Mary Paleologos said, "We lose our sense of wonder as we become adults."[1] She says, "Our need to know the outcome has taken precedent in our lives so much so that we are missing the magic of life. We are not comfortable with surprises and things that happen that we don't understand. We do not allow the magic of life to unfold."[2]

I can hear it now:

"Peter, where's Jesus? We need to find out where we're going to sleep tonight!"

"Hang on, Nathaniel. Lazarus died, so Jesus is bringing him back

---

1 Mary Paleologos, "A Sense of Wonder," *Huffington Post*, September 18, 2014, updated October 18, 2014, accessed March 14, 2017, http://www.huffingtonpost.com/mary-paleologos/a-sense-of-wonder_b_5686811.html.
2 Ibid.

to life."

"Oh, brother. How long do you think that'll take? I'm exhausted!"

Paleologos says we regain our wonder by allowing life to happen to us instead of making life happen. When difficult circumstances arise we ask not *how do I get out of this,* but *what can I learn from this?*

Exceptional theology, except that it lacks, well, Jesus. Add Jesus and everything changes.

When I imagine the campfire scenes in the days of Christ, I picture the disciples and followers leaning in and hanging on every word. I doubt they ever lost their sense of wonder, for most of the twelve and untold amounts of others through the ages followed Jesus to their own demise, martyred for their faith.

You see, Christ, God in the flesh, has the power to make the mundane marvelous, the trivial tremendous, and the ordinary extraordinary.

How does He do it?

One moment at a time as we seek Him in His Word, the Bible.

A large chunk of Scripture that has always struck me with wonder is the Gospel of John, chapters 13–17.

The night that the Pharisees arrested Jesus, He and the disciples had a long dinner table discussion that began with a foot washing.

They ate the Passover meal and then Jesus began to discuss the forthcoming events. He predicts Judas's betrayal, Peter's denial, and severe persecution. But tucked in the middle of the discourse is a beautiful promise:

> These things I have spoken to you while abiding with you. But the Helper, the Holy Spirit, whom the Father will send in My name, He will teach you all things, and bring to your remembrance all that I said to you. Peace I leave with you; My peace I give to you; not as the world gives do I give to you. Do not let your heart be troubled, nor let it be fearful.
>
> —John 14:25–27

I have tested these words and found them faithful and true.

As an avid reader of the Bible since seventh grade, I've learned God has been faithful to guide and direct me through His Word along the way. As you will read in the pages to come, He has reminded me of His faithfulness through hiking boots, glow sticks, and water skies. He has taught me grace and compassion through a book report, a cabbage, and my daughter's secret admirer.

The one who said "Let there be light" still speaks and has much to say to you. As you spend time in Scripture, the Holy Spirit will bring the words of Christ to mind at the opportune time in unexpected ways. Through boots, birds, and bicycles; through nature, art, and science.

God is the God of Wonder, and a life spent following Jesus is an extraordinary life, indeed.

Come and meet the God who makes the ordinary *extraordinary*.

THE BROKEN ANKLE

For just as each of us has one body with many members, and these members do not all have the same function, so in Christ we, though many, form one body, and each member belongs to all the others.

—Romans 12:4–5 NIV

I blame the boots.

In my defense, they were *fabulous* boots.

Grey suede faux leather (I'm cheap when it comes to trendy things) with a furry lining that folded over the laces. Four-inch-heeled hiking boots, and baby, I felt *fierce*.

My sister calls them a "statement piece." You know what I mean. The kind of clothing item that makes you stand a little bit taller, walk with a bit more swagger, and feel like you've hung the moon.

So there I was in the security line at Denver International Airport, fresh off a true mountaintop experience. There were ten of us on the power retreat—all ministry-minded women with a heart for Jesus and a dream of reaching His daughters through conferences and events.

I must have been thinking of them when I fell.

I should back up.

If you've never flown out of Denver, allow me to be the first to give you this gem: Give yourself plenty of time. Because there is only one security checkpoint for all of the gates, a two-hour wait is not unheard of.

The line moves steadily, if not slowly, but once you get to the conveyor belt, it's time to move. The TSA agents don't mess around, filing you through as quickly as possible. Once your bag is scanned, you're out.

So there I was in the security line at Denver International Airport, nervously eyeing the time. My plane was scheduled to begin boarding in fifteen minutes, but I had hoped to grab a snack first.

My turn came, and the race began: coat off, boots off, jewelry in a separate bowl, laptop has to be out of the bag, push the purse through last, and the requisite "no-ma'am-I'm-sorry-I-didn't-know-there-were-three-and-a-half-ounces-in-my-lotion-yes-you-can-throw-it-out" response to the question about the rogue bottle I missed in my carry-on.

Finally I was through and then came the awkward *where do I go to put my stuff back on* moment. There were only two chairs, and they were taken, so I took a few steps back and began to reassemble myself.

By the time I got to the boots, I was silently cursing myself for choosing fashion over ease, but it was too late. I bent down, laced up my right boot, and straightened back up. With nothing to hold on to, this would be tricky, but I certainly wasn't going to sit on the dirty airport floor.

I stood on my right leg, wobbling a bit as I tried to put the left boot on.

That's when I fell.

SNAP!

It felt as though the air had been sucked out of my chest. I had been standing, courtesy of the heels, four full inches off the ground. When I fell, I didn't so much as fall *down*, but rather fell *off* my boot. My ankle was now resting on the ground with my foot sideways on the floor.

Honestly, I don't know what was worse—the pain or the sound.

Not sure what would happen, I gingerly got myself up and tested my ankle.

Well, I can put weight on it, I thought to myself, *so it can't be broken.*

Two and a half weeks later, when the pain had intensified to the point where I was waking up at night, I went to the doctor and discovered I was wrong.

"When did you say you did this?" the doctor asked.

"December thirtieth," I replied.

He and the nurse exchanged glances.

He looked at me again, this time over the top of his glasses with a furrowed brow. "And you've been walking on it all this time?"

I cleared my throat nervously. "Um, well, yes."

"Look at this," he said and proceeded to trace the fine line that had neatly divided my bone in two.

I left thirty minutes later, the proud owner of a sturdy brace, a photocopied paper of stretches and exercises, and a bruised ego. By refusing to go to the doctor earlier and get the help I needed when I needed it, I had made a bigger mess of things.

Limping for two weeks had thrown out my lower back and taken a toll on my hip. *It's amazing,* I thought, *how one tiny little bone can have such a profound effect on the rest of my body.*

What is true for us is true for the Body of Christ—the Church.

It encourages me in a strange way, and it should encourage you, too. The apostle Paul, when addressing the Corinthian church, told the new Christians to think of themselves as one body with many parts. And in the eyes of Christ, no one part is more important than any other.

> Now if the foot should say, "Because I am not a hand, I do not belong to the body," it would not for that reason stop being part of the body. And if the ear should say, "Because I am not an eye, I do not belong to the body," it would not for that reason stop being part of the body. If the whole body were an eye, where would the sense of hearing be? If the whole body were an ear, where would the sense of smell be? But in fact God has placed the parts in the body, every one of them, just as he wanted them to be. If they were all one part, where would the body be? As it is, there are many parts, but one body.
>
> —1 Corinthians 12:15–20

As members of the Body of Christ, we have been uniquely gifted. Maybe you have the gift of encouragement, or perhaps your skills lie in administration. Do you love opening your home to others or making meals for the sick? You may have the gift of hospitality. God has planted all kinds of abilities in His children, each one interconnected to the others. Ephesians 4:16 says "From Him (Jesus) the whole body, joined and held together by every supporting ligament, grows and builds itself up in love, as each part does its work."

Your life's purpose lies in discovering how you fit into the Body and serving in the area of your giftedness.

That tiny broken bone ended up costing me six weeks of reduced activity. One little bone—so small and obscure that you need a professional to point it out to you, and yet my entire body felt the effects of its injury.

Consider this: If you are not working or serving the Body of Christ in your gifting, the Body cannot function optimally. You are denying your brothers and sisters of all the good you have to offer.

You are also denying yourself of a tremendous support system.

One of the women from Denver called me a few days after I'd found out about my ankle. I was on her heart, she said, and she wanted to make sure I was okay. One question turned into a forty-five minute conversation wrapped in laughter, love, and therapy.

"You know, you have to tell the other girls about this," she said.

She was right. I was playing hurt, and I desperately needed their prayers and encouragement.

When I turned my ankle the rest of my body made immediate adjustments to ease the burden on my broken bone.

Because that's what the Body does.

We work together, grow together, support one another, and carry each other's loads. We laugh together, rejoice together, suffer together, and make adjustments when a member is hurting.

No matter who you are or what you do, your gifts are too precious not to share, and the Body cannot function properly without you.

> And let us consider how we may spur one another on toward love and good deeds, not giving up meeting together, as some are in the habit of doing, but encouraging one another—and all the more as you see the Day approaching.
>
> —Hebrews 10:24–25

THE MISDIAGNOSIS

It started with a sore throat.

At first, it was an irritation: noticeable, but not worth mentioning. Then he started to complain.

"Go to the doctor," instructed his wife, but he didn't.

When the complaining outgrew her patience, she made the appointment for him.

The general practitioner checked his vitals and felt his lymph nodes: Swollen on one side, but not alarmingly so. His throat looked red—not unusual for springtime in Texas. With a flourish of scribble only a pharmacist could decipher, the doctor wrote a prescription for antibiotics and sent him on his way.

Diagnosis #1: Allergies

After ten days of antibiotics and only marginal improvement, back to the doctor he went.

"Hmm," said the GP, as he peered, prodded, and poked. "Why don't we send you to an ENT?"

The ears, nose, and throat specialist noticed something new—an inflamed right tonsil. Perhaps it was tonsillitis.

Diagnosis #2: Tonsillitis

"A tonsillectomy is terribly painful for a man your age," he said. "Let's try a stronger antibiotic before we resort to taking them out."

Eager to avoid surgery, the man agreed.

Four weeks and one antibiotic later, the man returned. This time, the tonsil had grown and so had the pain. No longer confined to his throat, the discomfort had traveled, lodging itself firmly in his inner ear.

The tonsil came out.

Then the labs came back.

The man, someone near and dear to my heart, had cancer.

The problem was not the antibiotics. Antibiotics are a reasonable solution. They just don't work on cancer.

The problem was not necessarily the cancer. This particular form of cancer caught early enough is rarely terminal. The man had an excellent prognosis: a 95 percent chance of a full recovery after six weeks of radiation.

The biggest problem was the misdiagnoses.

No one argued that the man had a problem. Where there is pain, there is often a problem.

The man was not without a solution. He tried antibiotics—twice—but when we fail to diagnose the problem, even the most time-tested solutions fail.

You and I have much in common with the man.

We have pain, and where there is pain, there's a problem.

We are not without solutions. A five-minute block of commercials wedged in the middle of our favorite program offers all kinds of quick fixes for all kinds of things. Bad hair? Pantene! Bad wrinkles? Botox! Feeling blue? New car! Feeling sluggish? Probiotics!

No, the argument isn't over whether or not there is a problem. Our symptoms bear witness that something is wrong: Restlessness, anxiety, feeling alone in a crowd. How about the failure to feel satisfaction at work? Or at home? Feelings of guilt, shame, or unworthiness—like our best is never enough.

We try one thing after another, and while "it" may work for a while, "it" ultimately leaves us a little more depressed than before.

King Solomon knew this well.

As a younger man, early in his kingship, the Lord gave him permission to ask for anything he wanted. Solomon chose well:

And Solomon said to God: "You have shown great and faithful love to my father David, and You have made me king in his place. Lord God, let Your promise to my father David now come true. For You have made me king over a people as numerous as the dust of the earth. Now grant me wisdom and knowledge so that I may lead these people, for who can judge this great people of Yours?"

—2 Chronicles 1:8–10 HCSB

Because Solomon chose wisdom over riches, God gave Him wisdom, riches, power, and fame. Later in life, Solomon performed a simple experiment: Try everything. See what happens.[3] Solomon spared no expense:

I increased my achievements. I built houses and planted vineyards for myself. I made gardens and parks for myself and planted every kind of fruit tree in them. I constructed reservoirs of water for myself from which to irrigate a grove of flourishing trees. I acquired male and female servants and had slaves who were born in my house. I also owned many herds of cattle and flocks, more than all who were before me in Jerusalem. I also amassed silver and gold for myself, and the treasure of kings and provinces. I gathered male and female singers for myself, and many concubines, the delights of men. So I became great and surpassed all who were before me in Jerusalem; my wisdom also remained with me. All that my eyes desired, I did not deny them. I did not refuse myself any pleasure, for I took pleasure in all my struggles. This was my reward for all my struggles.

—Ecclesiastes 2:4–10

At the conclusion of his experiment, he documented his results:

When I considered all that I had accomplished and what I had labored to achieve, I found everything to be futile and a

---

3 Ecclesiastes 2:1–3

pursuit of the wind. There was nothing to be gained under the sun.

—Ecclesiastes 2:11

He had everything, tried everything, did *everything*. Fame? Check. Money? Check. Women? Check.

Every solution, every fix, every *thing* under the sun—all futile, like chasing after the wind.

Funny thing about chasing the wind—you never catch it.

Solomon started well, but the money, fame, women, and things lured him away from the Lord, as they tend to do. That's when he developed—and misdiagnosed—his problem.

Jeremiah gives us the great diagnostic verse in all of Scripture:

The heart is more deceitful than all else and is desperately sick; who can understand it?

—Jeremiah 17:9 NASB

The prophet points out that, at the heart of it all, it's the heart that is sick. The vast majority of our problems are merely symptoms of a disease far worse than the worst of cancers, and that is the sin within.

We don't need a fix. We need a Physician.

Not just any physician. We need a Doctor with empathy, one who has walked where we walk, who knows rejection and loneliness. We need a Comforter with an excellent bedside manner, one who weeps when we weep and dries our tears. We need an Advocate who will intercede on our behalf. We need a miracle-worker, an on-the-water walker, and a storm-calmer; a sight-restorer, a leper-healer, and a dead-raiser.

He must be patient, for we are slow to learn; merciful, for we make mistakes; and loving when we are hard to love. Above all else, He must specialize in total heart transformation and mind regeneration.

Jesus is all of those things. He sees your worst and gives His best. You don't have to clean up your act before you come to Him. No one waits until they are well to visit the doctor. Remember the woman caught in the act of adultery? John 8:1–11 paints a painful picture. In her moment of greatest weakness and vulnerability, she is caught both physically and metaphorically naked.

Dragged from the bed, through the town, and thrown before her soon-to-be Savior.

While the Pharisees are quick to condemn, Jesus would have none of it. "If anyone of you is without sin, let him be the first to throw a stone at her."

When the last one leaves, Jesus looks up, speaks love, and sends her on her way.

Why? Because only the love of a Savior can save a sinner.

Back to the cancer. The man began an intense six-week schedule of radiation, five days on, two days off. Three months later he was cancer free. The high-energy radiation blasted the cancer cells, destroying their ability to divide and multiply, ultimately freeing up the healthy cells to reproduce.

The love of Christ is stronger than the strongest radiation, for it can mend your heart, save your life, and change your mind. The symptoms of our sinful condition are dire but treatable. You can know peace. You can feel joy. You can rest knowing that the God of the Universe has pledged to meet your needs.

Through Jesus you can be, once and for all eternity, fully healed and made whole.

> Jesus said to her, "I am the resurrection and the life. The one who believes in Me, even if he dies, will live. Everyone who lives and believes in Me will never die—ever. Do you believe this?"
>
> "Yes, Lord," she told Him, "I believe You are the Messiah, the Son of God, who comes into the world."
>
> —John 11:25–27 HCSB

FLOOR SEATS

And the angel said to me, "Write this: Blessed are those who are invited to the wedding feast of the Lamb." And he added, "These are true words that come from God."

—Revelation 19:9 NLT

For my husband, Mike, Wednesday, November 20th, 2013, was a day for the history books.

That was the day the Dallas Mavericks were scheduled to play the Houston Rockets at home.

That was also the day he got floor seats.

I was enjoying a lovely lunch with some girlfriends when my phone rang. A glance told me it was Mike. Knowing I was leaving in minutes, I declined the call.

It rang again.

Mike doesn't call twice in a row unless something is really wrong or really good. Praying for the latter, I answered the phone.

The next sixty seconds was an excited stream of words-tripping-over-words, but I was able to make out "Mavs game," "tonight," and "floor seats."

"I know it's last minute and I know you're tired, but do you care if I go?"

Yes. I'm going to stop you from going to a big game. I'm going to stop you from sitting on the same surface that graces the soles of Dirk Nowitski's Nikes. I'm going to keep you from floor seats.

"Are you kidding me? You have to go!"

Although only one of us was going, both of us were thrilled. Now don't get me wrong, God has blessed us tremendously and we are thankful for all that we have, but floor seats? That's not how we roll.

Being a morning radio gal, I am typically up a good three hours before the rest of the house. As I turned off my alarm clock the next morning I noticed a text message.

It was a picture of Mike. On Fox. In floor seats.

Later that day my husband filled me in on the details.

The ticket was a gift from a friend named Mark Thompson. Mr. Thompson is the President/CEO of a very big company. The very big company is a corporate sponsor of the Dallas Mavericks.

When you are the president of the company that sponsors a team, you get floor seats.

But that's not all.

My husband met Mark at a restaurant before the game. Mark suggested they ride to the stadium together. Because Mark is a Mavs VIP, he parks in a special parking lot underground. When they go in, they walk down a long hall to the VIP lounge.

At the VIP lounge my husband ate from the VIP buffet, drank a Diet Coke from the VIP bar, and hobnobbed with other VIPs.

Shortly before the game started they walked down another long hall lined with cheerleaders stretching before taking the court. Then they walked out onto the floor and took their seats.

Their *floor* seats.

Mike made a big point of thanking Mark both that night and the next day on Facebook as he posted pictures. You see, my husband knows that it was not his name that got him in the door.

It was Mark's.

Because he knows Mark, he parked like a VIP, ate like a VIP, talked with the VIPs, and enjoyed the game from floor seats, *on Mark's invitation*. You are I are also the recipients of an invitation—a *heavenly* invitation.

> There is more than enough room in my Father's home. If this were not so, would I have told you that I am going to prepare a place for you? When everything is ready, I will come and get you, so that you will always be with me where I am.
>
> —John 14:2–3

Friend, let's be honest. Life can be brutal. Violence is everywhere. Natural disasters kill thousands a year and uproot millions more. Jobs disappoint us, people betray us, and our bodies fail us. Most of us are accustomed to operating in a state of constant low-grade anxiety. Psychologist and anxiety specialist Dr. Richard Leahy says, "The average high school kid today has the same level of anxiety as the average psychiatric patient in the early 1950s."[4]

Something's gotta give.

Fortunately, Someone did.

Over two thousand years ago, Jesus Christ gave His perfect, precious, sinless life so that you, a sinner, could have Heavenly Floor Seats.

God is perfectly sinless. We are perfectly sinful. On our best day we still fall short. Our name will never get us through the pearly gates.

The good news is this: We don't give our name at the door. We give His.

We get to heaven based on *His* work on the cross. We sit at the heavenly banquet on His ticket. We get heavenly room and board because *He* paid the price. We have access to the throne room of God because Jesus says, "See this one? This one is mine. This one is with Me."

And because of Him we have hope. Because we have hope we can rejoice, even in the midst of our worst trials.

Because there is more.

Because what you are going through right now is not it for you.

If you are in Jesus, you roll VIP.

Do you know Him? Do you trust Him? Have you allowed him access to your heart?

Have you given Him your life?

Don't wait another moment.

He longs for you. He lived for you. He died *for you.*

Oh, that you would know Him and live.

Who then will condemn us? No one—for Christ Jesus died

---

4 Tullian Tchividjian, "One Way Love," (Colorado Springs, CO: David C. Cook, 2013), 19.

for us and was raised to life for us, and he is sitting in the place of honor at God's right hand, pleading for us.

—Romans 8:34

SPIRITUAL DETOX

Detox:

Syllabification: de·tox
Verb: Abstain from or rid the body of toxic or unhealthy substances.[5]

I am not one to jump on the fad bandwagon. I was the last girl in my sorority to own a pair of Birkenstocks. Remember when boot-cut turned into the resurgence of bell-bottoms? They had probably gone the way of the '70s by the time I bought my first pair on a clearance rack marked 80 percent off. Uggs had been gracing the feet of celebrities and the pages of magazines a full decade before I surrendered (love 'em). I still maintain yoga pants are strictly for yoga, and it was 2016 before I owned a pair of ankle boots.

In other words, you probably wouldn't accuse me of being trendy.

Except with the detox cleanse.

As soon as my girlfriends started talking about it I was in.

It sounded so good, so simple. Three days of no food, no caffeine, and no soda. Any time you feel hungry or thirsty, you drink a strange concoction of water, lemon, ginger, and something greenish, and when you're done you have completely rid yourself of impurities and toxins.

---

5 Oxford Dictionary, s.v. "detox," http://www.oxforddictionaries.com/us/definition/american_english/detox.

31

They also said it gave you younger looking skin.

Say no more.

I picked up the supplies from the grocery store and stared uncertainly at the small pile of ingredients that was supposed to sustain me for the next three days. A period of time, by the way, that sounded much shorter when my girlfriend was enthusiastically boasting of the detoxification benefits.

So I did it.

Until ten o'clock that morning.

By 10:00 a.m. the hunger pains were nearly as sharp as the withdrawal headache hammering away at my skull as my body angrily protested the caffeine depravation.

Detoxing is for the birds, I thought to myself as I grabbed a cup of coffee and a bagel.

I thought about the detox cleanse one morning as I was journaling.

We can detox our bodies so easily, I scribbled. *How do we detox our minds?*

The jury is out on how much good a detox actually does. God created our bodies in such a manner that, when stewarded properly, they are literal detox machines. Our minds are far more complicated.

> Let us not become boastful, challenging one another, envying one another.
>
> —Galatians 5:26 NASB

As I journaled, writing furiously as though I could exfoliate my mind through my pen, I repented of the thing that was weighing me down.

It started with a Facebook post.

She had scored a victory: a big, fat, juicy, hard-earned win.

She was a casual acquaintance, and I paused before I posted a congratulatory comment.

I paused because I was ashamed. You see, my first thought—the very first emotion that bubbled up inside of me—was not delight.

It was disappointment. Before I could stop myself, I had compared my lot to hers, my achievements to hers, and finding mine lacking, I felt resentful and discouraged.

Nearly a lifetime of knowing and loving the Lord, over three decades of reading His Word, and my first thought was tinged green with envy.

I hate that part of me.

I hate telling you about that part of me even more.

Per 2 Corinthians 10:5, I immediately confessed, begged God's forgiveness, and asked Him to take the ugly thought captive "to make it obedient to Christ."

But that doesn't change the fact that it was there. Jeremiah 17:9 says, "The heart is more deceitful than all else and is desperately sick; who can understand it?" Not me. Not any of us, if we were to drop the masks and show our true colors. The ancient prophet has diagnosed my condition correctly. The fleshy muscle that pumps my blood doubles as a sin generator, and because of this, I have to wrestle those ugly thoughts to the ground when they pop up.

I can confess this to you because, although you might not say it out loud, this is a fight that you know, too.

The apostle Paul outlined our battle strategy in his second letter to the church at Corinth:

> For though we live in the world, we do not wage war as the world does. The weapons we fight with are not the weapons of the world. On the contrary, they have divine power to demolish strongholds. We demolish arguments and every pretension that sets itself up against the knowledge of God, and we take captive every thought to make it obedient to Christ.
>
> —2 Corinthians 10:3–5

Don't miss the weight of this passage. Paul says take every thought captive.

Every thought. Captive. And *make* it obey Christ.

Our thoughts don't want to obey Christ, do they? Mine don't. My thoughts want to dwell on my hurts, my mistakes, and my failures. They want to "fantasy-fight" with the one that wounded me. They want to relive that which should be left behind and reopen that which has been healed.

How I wish they would stop. How I beg God for reprieve. I want to be free from the power of the flesh and cleansed from every impure thought.

I need a full-on spiritual detox.

> Make them holy by your truth; teach them your word, which is truth.
>
> —John 17:17 NLT

I spent nearly thirty minutes in my journal that morning, asking the Lord to use whatever means necessary to stop the sin-generator inside of me. Finally, with tears in my eyes and a cramp in my hand, I laid down my pen and opened my Bible.

That's when God spoke.

> Therefore there is now no condemnation for those who are in Christ Jesus.
>
> —Romans 8:1 NASB

And it hit me like a holy Mack truck.

No matter what you do, no matter what you say, no matter what you *think*, if you are in Christ, then God stubbornly refuses to condemn you.

There is risk in my confession. You could throw this book away. You could talk about me behind my back. You could stand at the feet of the Father and accuse me and condemn me for hours, but God never will.

How crazy is that?

No matter how mucky and grimy I get, He won't condemn. Convict, yes. Condemn, no.

Never.

You know what that makes me do?

It makes me love Him.

It makes me want to follow Him.

It makes me want to obey Him.

It gives me a genuine sense of delight for my casual acquaintance and her big win.

The knowledge of His love sanitizes my heart. The churchy word for that is "sanctify."

In John 17, the great High Priestly prayer, Jesus begs the Father to cleanse, detoxify, and sanctify us, and the scrub brush of choice is His Word.

According to Micah 7:18, when you fall He delights to show you mercy. Lamentations 3:22 reminds us that we cannot drain Him of compassion, for each sunrise brings a fresh batch of mercy. According to Ephesians 1:1–10, you are chosen, forgiven, redeemed, and blessed with every spiritual blessing in Christ. He casts your sin as far as the east is from the west and never calls it to mind again (Ps. 103:12).

As long as you and I wear a cloak of skin, we will struggle against fleshly thoughts and desires. That's okay. The one who says she doesn't struggle with her thoughts is the one who has stopped fighting to corral them into obedience.

Fight on, knowing that the Lord of all creation, the Lord of Hosts, the Alpha and the Omega, the King above all kings has dug in His heels and stubbornly refuses to condemn you.

Not only that, but He stubbornly refuses to quit on you.

He stubbornly insists on loving you—on looking at you through the lens of compassion, and draping you in the clothing of salvation.

Let that wash over and through you. Drink it in daily, and let the spiritual detox begin.

> Dear friends, you always followed my instructions when I was with you. And now that I am away, it is even more important. Work hard to show the results of your salvation, obeying God with deep reverence and fear. For God is working in you, giving you the desire and the power to do what pleases him.
>
> —Philippians 2:12–13 NLT

GRAY LEGGINGS AND GRACE

Lo, for my own welfare I had great bitterness; It is You who has kept my soul from the pit of nothingness, For You have cast all my sins behind Your back.

—Isaiah 38:17 NASB

It all started with the black leggings.

The elementary school my children attend has a policy when it comes to shorts. It's a policy I wholeheartedly affirm—if the shorts are too short, the kids wear leggings. Because the stores only seem to carry what I call "shorty-shorts," my nine-year-old daughter has quite a collection of stretch pants.

One day, Caitlyn came home from school with a tear in the knee of her black leggings.

Not a big deal. Not unusual, either. My kids are not allowed to play on electronics during the week, so that means when homework is finished, they head outside, not to be seen again until dinner time—a lifestyle that takes its toll on their clothes.

I commented on the sizable hole, and asked my daughter a simple question: "Honey, why don't you go put on another pair?"

"I can't, Mom! They all have holes in them and the pink ones are too small."

Further investigation on my part confirmed this to be true, so the next day I stopped by the store. All stretch pants were on sale for ten dollars, so I picked up two pairs—one gray, one black—and headed back to the house.

After school, my daughter squealed with delight. "Gray ones!

Thank you, Mommy! I've never had gray ones before!"

Smiling at how easy it was to make her day, I began to prepare dinner.

Moments later she returned, proudly modeling her two-hour-old, brand-new pair of gray leggings. Then she raced off to play.

"Not so fast," I hollered. "Come back inside and change your clothes."

"Please, Mommy, can I please, *please* wear them this once? I won't tear them, I swear!"

"Caitlyn, those are school clothes. If you are going to be running around outside I want you in play clothes."

After a minute or two of listening to a stream of "I promise" and "we're playing inside," I relented.

"But Caitlyn, listen to me. Look me right in the eyes."

She turned back around, her sweet grin reaching from ear to ear.

"If you ruin your new pants, I will not buy you new ones."

With an "I love you" and an "I promise," she raced out of the house, slamming the door behind her.

Not twenty minutes passed before I heard the door creak open.

"Mommy?"

"Hi, honey! I thought you were over at Jocelyn's house."

"Well, um, I'm going back over in a minute but I wanted to come tell you the truth."

I looked up from the salad I'd been fixing.

"I swear I didn't mean to, Mommy."

I held my gaze on hers.

"I swear I didn't mean to, Mommy!"

Against my specific instructions, she and her friend had decided to ride scooters. Caitlyn had run into a bush, caught her leggings, and torn a large hole in the derrière.

> As a father has compassion on his children, so the LORD
> has compassion on those who fear Him. For He knows what
> we are made of, remembering that we are dust.
>
> —Psalm 103:13–14 HCSB

My two children respond to discipline differently. My playful Nick is the one to push the boundaries as far as he can. Caitlyn, my little rule-follower, needs only a sharp glance to keep her in line.

I expressed disbelief first, then disappointment, and watched as my little girl crumbled.

What followed was unexpected.

My daughter spiraled down into a self-defeating state of self-loathing, crying that she hated herself and that she could "never do anything right." An hour later she was still sobbing in her bedroom, absolutely inconsolable.

In part, because she had been very excited about the leggings, but also because she has a tender heart that longs to please.

I pulled Caitlyn onto my lap and held her tightly as she cried. Finally, I turned her face toward mine, wiped her tears, and kissed her wet cheeks.

"Sweetheart," I said softly, "you are nine years old."

"I should know better!" she yelled, her voice hoarse from crying.

"Caitlyn, listen to me. You are nine years old. Mommy expects you to make mistakes."

Tightening my hug, I continued. "I am never surprised when you make mistakes. But I do expect you to learn from them. Now you need to make a choice. Are you going to let this one little thing ruin your entire night, or are you going to take what you've learned and make the right choice next time?"

A few more minutes of snuggling and she ran off in her ripped up stretch pants. I made my way back to the kitchen, thinking about our exchange, and how it applies to you and me.

How many times have you let the instant rewind machine in your mind pull out the footage of your past and play it on repeat? How many times have you allowed yesterday to tarnish today? How many of your ghosts are living rent-free in your head?

Friend, what I said to my daughter applies to us. Our Heavenly Father knows we are frail. He knows we will fall and He knows we will fail. He has already accommodated for that. The work on the cross took into account every sin you would ever commit.

Your addictions.

Your insecurities.

Your iniquities.

Your short fuse and your hot temper.

All of it. Paid in full and non-refundable.

You have not made your last mistake, told your last lie, or failed for the last time. Is that an excuse to continue in sin?

A thousand times, *no*!

It is a precious reminder of our desperate need for a never ending river of forgiveness, and the beautiful realization that the river is always there.

I did not buy my daughter a new pair of pants. I love her too much to do that. I care too much about her long-term character to keep her from the sting of the consequences. Mistakes are the best teachers we have. But here is what you and I must always remember:

Our failures are a teaching tool, not a prison cell.

The prophet Micah describes our Heavenly Father as one who delights to show mercy, who casts our transgression into the sea, never to be retrieved.

Let's stop deep-sea fishing and swim in the river instead.

THE BOOK REPORT

For the LORD takes delight in his people; he crowns the humble with victory.

—Psalm 149:4 NIV

Do you remember your first book report? I haven't the faintest recollection of mine, but I will never forget my son's.

Nick was a seven-year-old first-grader when he brought the assignment home. It was as simple as you would expect a first-grade book report to be:

- Select a book from home or the library.

- Answer four questions.

- Don't forget to write your name in the top right corner.

- Turn in on Friday.

The project came home on a Monday. Nick's library day was Wednesday. Not wanting him to select a book he had already read, I told him to pick one out at school, bring it home, and we would work on it together that afternoon.

Now for a moment of context.

The book report assignment came home while I was in the middle of an intense period of preparation. At the beginning stages of writing lessons for a women's retreat, I was studying everything I could get my hands on having to do with ancient Israel.

One day my son and I were snuggling on the couch and found a documentary on—you guessed it—ancient Israel. As the show's host guided our tour, I would periodically comment on how much I would love to travel to the country one day and walk in the footsteps of Christ.

Back to the book report.

Tuesday night, as I tucked my children into bed, I reminded my son to pick a book for his assignment.

Wednesday afternoon, as the kids climbed into the car, it was the first thing out of his mouth:

"Mom, I got a book and you're going to love it!"

"I can't wait to see it, honey, but let's wait until we get home."

Once the snack was eaten and my daughter was settled with her math, I turned to Nick.

"Okay, buddy, let's see what you picked!"

Crumpled papers and crumbs tumbled out of his backpack as he fumbled for the book. Glimpsing the cover, my eyes immediately filled with tears as a lump swelled in the back of my throat.

"Look, Mom, it's on Israel," he proudly exclaimed.

I slowly turned it over in my hands. It was a textbook, not a storybook, roughly two inches thick. The font was smaller than his seven-year-old eyes were used to, and there were far more words than pictures.

"What made you choose this book, buddy?"

"It's a God book," he said, puzzled at my reaction. "Plus, I knew you'd like it."

Be still, my heart.

My sweet son had thought of me. While he was combing through the aisles of brightly colored covers, he bypassed *Frog and Toad*, *The Doug Chronicles*, *Junie B. Jones*, and *The Dork Diaries* to choose a book for one reason alone: to please me.

"I love it," I whispered as I caught him up in a bear-hug, "I just *love* it."

> His pleasure is not in the strength of the horse, nor his delight in the legs of the warrior; the LORD delights in those who fear him, who put their hope in his unfailing love.
>
> —Psalm 147:10–11

Did my son's book choice make me love him more? No. In fact, that is not even in the realm of the possible, because my love for both Caitlyn and Nick has nothing to do with their behavior and everything to do with their identity. They are *mine*, and my love for them is unchangeable. But when they think of me, when they seek to please me, my heart nearly bursts with delight.

I hope that brings you a measure of peace. This is how your Heavenly Father loves you.

Your good works can't make Him love you more, just as your sin can't make Him love you less. His love for you is not connected to your behavior.

I'd like you to read that one more time.

His love for you is not connected to your behavior. His love for you is not affected by your love for Him or lack thereof. It is not connected to your faithfulness or your faithlessness, your selflessness or selfishness; nor does it hinge on how often you go to church, how much you read your Bible, or how much money you give.

His love for you has nothing to do with *what* you do and everything to do with *who you are*.

If you are in Christ, you are His. Completely, irrevocably, inexorably His, and when God's children seek to please their Heavenly Father, His heart overflows with delight.

My children make plenty of mistakes. They push their boundaries and test my patience. They fight, they holler, and they can turn a clean house into a disaster zone in less time than it takes me to cook dinner.

It doesn't shock me. I expect it. It is part of the growth process. And because I am a loving mom, I discipline them. Not to punish, but to correct and instruct.

You have and will make plenty of mistakes. You will push your boundaries and test His patience. You will sin accidentally and sometimes deliberately. You will silence His whispers and ignore His nudges.

He is not shocked by this. He saw it coming, which is why all of us need a Savior. And because He is a loving Father, He disciplines us. Not to punish, but to correct and instruct; to bring you closer to Him, that you might know Him better and discover the joy only found in obedience. The more you know this joy, the more you'll seek to please Him.

And you *do* please Him, not because of you, because of Christ. But when you choose His will over your way, you delight Him.

Ultimately, Nick picked a different book. But later, as we sat flipping through his first choice, he turned to me and asked, "Can I take you to Israel someday, Mom?"

Tears threatened to spill down my cheeks and smudge my mascara.

"You bet you can, buddy. We will go to Israel someday, and I will show you all the places where Jesus walked."

"Will we see Him there?"

"No. But we'll feel Him."

Oh, be still, my heart.

> The Lord your God is with you, the Mighty Warrior who saves. He will take great delight in you; in his love he will no longer rebuke you, but will rejoice over you with singing.
>
> —Zephaniah 3:17–18

THE CABBAGE

Cursed is the ground because of you; in toil you will eat of it all the days of your life.

—Genesis 3:17b NASB

Bill and Coral Brittain have the best yard of anyone in our little neighborhood in Flower Mound, Texas. It is quite fitting, in fact, that they live in Flower Mound, because they have the most beautiful flowers of anyone I know.

Their yard is perfectly manicured, their trees are perfectly pruned, and their flowers are, well, *perfect*.

We, on the other hand, don't fare quite so well in our landscaping.

Don't get me wrong—my husband does a beautiful job with the lawn. He keeps the trees and shrubs in check, but the flowers have been left to me.

Which is why we don't have any.

Oh, we plant them every year, to be sure.

It's just that they die.

"Plant perennials," you would tell me if we were face-to-face. "Plant something hardy, like geraniums."

Been-there-done-that on both accounts. Nothing seems to work.

"Plant sweet-potato vine," said my friend Amanda. "You can't kill that if you try!"

Oh yes I can, my friend. And I did.

One day I asked Bill his secret.

"Texas soil is awful," he said, shaking his head. "If you want your plants to thrive, you have to first test the soil to see what you're dealing with. You live right behind us, so I can save you the trouble. You're not going to grow anything in the dirt you're sitting on."

My eyes widened as a glimmer of hope rose to the surface. You mean I wasn't at fault? I wasn't a natural-born-flower-killer?

"I have been using organic soil for years," he continued. "I won't use anything else."

He went on to list a certain type of food that escapes me, along with a few more tricks of the trade.

Fast forward two years to the cabbage.

I sat in the carpool lane of my kids' elementary school, sinking lower and lower into my seat. One child after another walked by laughing and chatting excitedly with their friends.

Some were holding a small plant in their hands. The ones with plants were third graders.

Oh no . . .

I knew exactly what that meant.

It meant that my daughter had an assignment that involved growing things.

Unfortunately for my daughter and her grades, she had a mom notorious for killing growing things.

Nick jumped in and broke the news first.

"Mom, look! Caitlyn has a cabbage that she has to grow for school!"

"Nick!" yelled Caitlyn through clenched teeth, "That's my news!"

After dinner she and I carefully went over the instructions. The plant was part of the Bonnie Cabbage Program, designed to teach the students about deferred gratification and the value of investing time and energy into something over a season.

There were two ways you could plant the cabbage: In your yard in a 3x3 foot area or in an 18–24 inch diameter pot.

We went for the pot.

That's when I remembered Bill's advice.

We bought the best organic soil we could find. We went online to bonniecabbageprogram.com to learn everything we could about proper care.

Then we waited.

I could not believe what happened next.

It grew.

That little cabbage grew and grew and grew and ten weeks later had completely filled the pot.

All because of the soil.

> But blessed are those who trust in the Lord and have made the Lord their hope and confidence. They are like trees planted along a riverbank, with roots that reach deep into the water. Such trees are not bothered by the heat or worried by long months of drought. Their leaves stay green, and they never stop producing fruit.
>
> —Jeremiah 17:7–8 NLT

Everything else I have ever planted *in my life* has started strong only to dry up and whither under less-than-ideal conditions. But the cabbage? I've never seen anything so hardy! It's made it through three or four freezes where we forgot to put it in the garage overnight. It has withstood several days in a row without sunlight when we forgot to take it *out* of the garage during a freeze. We've forgotten to feed it, forgotten to water it, forgotten *about* it, and yet it prevails.

This leads me to ask you an important question: what are you rooted and established in?

> I pray that out of his glorious riches he may strengthen you with power through his Spirit in your inner being, so that Christ may dwell in your hearts through faith. And I pray that you, being rooted and established in love, may have power, together with all the Lord's holy people, to grasp how wide and long and high and deep is the love of Christ, and to know this love that surpasses knowledge—that you may be filled to the measure of all the fullness of God.
>
> —Ephesians 3:16–19 NIV

God desires so much more for us than to merely exist. If your life consists of waking up, managing house/kid duties, punching in, punching out, and going to bed, know this:

You are missing God's best for you.

Glance back at Ephesians 3—the apostle Paul petitions the Father that, out of His glorious riches, you would be strengthened and empowered with the very same power that raised Christ from the grave. Why? To trudge through each day with a low grade of frustration and depression?

No way.

You were made for more. Much more.

God chose you, saved you, and empowers you to thrive.

He has gifted and equipped you to do great work, work that produces good fruit. But as my black thumb would testify, the soil is essential for the fruit.

Plant yourself in the good, rich soil of God's love. Paul suggests that the love of Christ is so vast that we have no chance of knowing it without His help. But as we seek to understand the depths of His love for us we will be "filled to the measure of all the fullness of God."

I want *that.*

How staggering that the Creator of the Universe would desire a relationship so intimate with us that it requires Him actually indwelling us.

So how do we do it?

We plant ourselves in the richness of His love by seeking to know it through worship, study, and gathering with other believers. According to John 15:9, we are to abide or remain in His love, and we do that by spending time with Christ every day in prayer. We feed ourselves the bread of His Word (Deut. 8:3) and drink deeply from the Living Water that is Jesus (John 4:13–14).

Simply put, we prioritize Him. We choose Him over lesser things. We trust Him with our brokenness and ask Him to strengthen our faith. We pray that He might expose areas of unbelief and replace them with trust.

We ask Him to make Himself the desire of our heart.

There is no higher pursuit than to seek His face. And when we do, we thrive.

Oh, the joys of those who do not follow the advice of the

wicked, or stand around with sinners, or join in with mockers. But they delight in the law of the Lord, meditating on it day and night. They are like trees planted along the riverbank, bearing fruit each season. Their leaves never wither, and they prosper in all they do.

—Psalm 1:1–3 NLT

THE MODEL PLANE

This is the book of the generations of Adam. In the day when God created man, He made him in the likeness of God.

—Genesis 5:1 NASB

I looked down at the pile of screws, nuts, and round things, and sighed. A model airplane kit for his seventh birthday. *This can't be for a seven-year-old*, I thought to myself, and looked at the box. Yep, ages 7+.

"Nick, are you sure you don't want to wait until Daddy is done working on his car?"

A pair of big, beautiful, woeful brown eyes looked up at me. The brows furrowed and the lip quivered, but it didn't matter. The eyes were my undoing.

"Okay, sweetie, hand Mommy the directions."

The two of us sat side by side, Nick in his element, me nowhere near mine. My son already had the first few pieces we needed; now it was time to build.

Slowly, methodically, we turned screws and attached round things. Proud of our work, I held it up and said, "Look Nick, we did it!"

An engineer in the making, Nick looked at the picture and looked at . . . whatever it was I had made. "Mommy," he wailed, "you did it backwards!"

Backwards, indeed. Undo screws and round things. Start over from scratch.

Just at that moment, my husband, fixer of all things big and small, walked in to check our progress.

"Okay, Nick," I said sheepishly, "I need a round thing, a square thing, and a little screw. No, not that one. The big square thing."

"That's also called a bolt," he said cheerfully, as he strode confidently over to our work-space.

"Here, buddy, let me take a look."

My husband looked at my . . . whatever, looked at the instructions, and turned to my son.

"Bud, you and I can do this together after dinner. It won't take us long, and I'd love to help you. Why don't we let Mommy go running and you and I will tackle this later?"

Satisfied with the solution, Nick moved on to something else.

"Thank you," I said. "He'd rather do it with you anyway."

> God created man in His own image, in the image of God He created him; male and female He created them.
>
> —Genesis 1:27

Later on that evening, I watched as my husband and his "mini-me," our son, huddled over the kitchen table. "Hand me a washer (round thing), bud. Now grab the flat screwdriver." Mike carefully explained each step, offered a demonstration, then handed it over to Nick.

Twenty short minutes later Nick came bounding into my bedroom. "Look, Mom! See? We did it! Dad knew how and he showed me. It was easy!"

I made the required amount of fuss, told him how proud I was of him, and sent him to get ready for bed. Nothing gives my husband more satisfaction that working hard and completing a project, and clearly, Nick was cut from the same cloth.

> For we are His workmanship, created in Christ Jesus for good works, which God prepared beforehand so that we would walk in them.
>
> —Ephesians 2:10

Mike walked in as I was brushing my teeth. "You know," he said, "that was really good time with Nick and me. This was the first I felt like he really listened to what I had to say."

I smiled around a mouthful of foam.

"I just have so much I want to teach him, you know?"

I did know. A few nights prior I had taken my daughter to a conference. As the host, I introduced the worship team, the speakers, and gave short snippets of testimony in between. Caitlyn, just eight years old, opened the conference with a blessing and accompanied me on stage each time. I have so much I want to teach her: so much of myself that I want to give to both her and her brother.

There is a reason we want to pass on part of ourselves to our children. God divinely designed us that way.

Genesis chapter 1 paints a sweeping, panoramic picture of creation. Seven times we read, "God said . . . and it was so." God speaks the heavens and the earth into existence. Light, land, water, vegetation, fish, birds—each time calling forth matter where, moments before, there had been none.

But with man, He does things differently.

> Then the Lord God formed the man out of the dust from the ground and breathed the breath of life into his nostrils, and the man became a living being.
>
> —Genesis 2:7 HCSB

God is Spirit, and thus without form, but the picture He illustrates for us is this: The Creator enters His creation. He confines Himself to time and space, enters the Garden, and kneels down. He takes His hands and gathers a pile of dust. With great care, He forms the shape of a man; pressing the earth down, molding and patting until Adam is complete.

How long did God look at His Son before He imparted a piece of His Spirit into him? What did that look like? Did He pull Adam into his arms? I imagine the Father looking at His child's face the same way you did when you held your sleeping infant. So peaceful. So innocent. So perfect.

In my mind I can see it: The Father smooths back his son's hair, tilts back his son's head, and blows the breath of life into man's nostrils, and Adam begins to breath.

Like Adam, you and I are covered in the handprints of God. And our spirit bears His likeness, too.

When God breathed into Adam, He passed on some of His characteristics. Before there was sin, there was love, joy, peace, patience, kindness, goodness, faithfulness, gentleness, and self-control—all bearing witness to His Spirit that lives in the heart of every believer.

Mike and I have no desires for our children outside of this: that they grow to love Jesus and grow in His likeness. But how delightful to see my daughter developing my quirky sense of humor and love for the stage. My husband beamed with pride when my son insisted on taking karate so he could be "just like Daddy!" We all long to pass a legacy of ourselves on to our children.

How precious, that the Creator of the Universe desires the same for you. Not because He has to, because He wants to. Because He loves you. Because you are His legacy, His witness, and the crown jewel of His Creation.

Because you are His.

> And we all, who with unveiled faces contemplate the Lord's glory, are being transformed into his image with ever-increasing glory, which comes from the Lord, who is the Spirit.
>
> —2 Corinthians 3:18 NIV

DEEPER WATERS

Great peace have those who love your law, and nothing can make them stumble.

—Psalm 119:165

One minute everything was fine. Life was moving along quite well. Work was good, marriage was good, kids were good.

Then the storm hit.

It started with the cancer diagnosis. Then severe depression invaded our inner circle. Then the foundation problems. Then the house flooded. Then the dog ruined every square inch of *brand new* carpet downstairs. Then the car needed thousands of dollars in repairs.

Like a boxer out his league, the blows kept coming, and there was nothing we could do to block them.

Have you been there? Where the waves are too high and the wind is too strong? Where the rain pelts your face until you can barely see?

A scuba diver recounts his experience of diving in a storm:

I plunged through the rolling waves. It was like being dropped into a pot of boiling water (without the heat, of course). Immediately I was disoriented.

But then something odd happened.

As I began to sink, things became clearer. The chaos seemed controlled. At 30 feet, it was motionless—crystal clear. It seemed as if I could see hundreds of feet in every direction.

By the time I hit 100 feet, I might as well have been on another planet. It was beyond magical. I've never experienced anything like it before or since. The chaos I had experienced on the water's surface was a distant memory.[6]

There is a lesson to be learned from the ocean, and our diver summarizes it well:

"The deeper you go, the calmer it gets."[7]

When we find ourselves in swirling circumstances, that is the time to go deep.

Deeper into His Presence.

Deeper into His Comfort.

Deeper into His Word.

When the waves are high and the wind is strong and our world is shaking around us, our natural tendency is to panic. When we panic we are vulnerable to depression and despondency. Panic can literally paralyze us.

Don't panic.

Go deep.

God is not surprised by your storm, your circumstances, or your situation. Every gale of wind that hits you must first pass through His hands, and if it passes through His hands *there is purpose in it.*

> You are being protected by God's power through faith for a salvation that is ready to be revealed in the last time. You rejoice in this, though now for a short time you have had to struggle in various trials so that the genuineness of your faith—more valuable than gold, which perishes though refined by fire—may result in praise, glory, and honor at the revelation of Jesus Christ.
>
> —1 Peter 1:5–7 HCSB

---

6 Robert D. Smith, "The Deeper You Go the Calmer It Gets," *Therobertd.com,* April, 29, 2014, accessed February 19, 2016, http://www.therobertd.com/the-deeper-you-go-the-calmer-it-gets/#sthash.zbpO1LXP.dpuf.
7 Ibid.

James Merritt writes about Korean Christians suffering horrific persecution because of their faith. They were known for saying, "We are like nails. The harder you hit us, the deeper you drive us; and the deeper you drive us, the more peaceful it becomes."[8]

When we dive deep into the Word of God we remember that, throughout history, the church and its saints have suffered every persecution known to man. The great apostle Paul was flogged, whipped, stoned, smuggled out of cities in baskets, and shipwrecked three times. Yet the cry of his heart was this:

> I want to know Christ and experience the mighty power that raised him from the dead. I want to suffer with him, sharing in his death, so that one way or another I will experience the resurrection from the dead!
>
> —Philippians 3:10–11 NLT

When the storms of life surround you, drive yourself deep into the Word of the only one who can comfort, the only one who can heal, and the only one who can bathe you in lasting peace.

Your Heavenly Father loves you. He still walks on water. He still parts the sea. He still calms the storms. And when the waves surge and the thunder roars, He invites you to swim in the deep.

---

8 James Merritt, *How to Be a Winner and Influence Anybody: The Fruit of the Spirit as the Essence of Leadership* (Camarillo, CA: Xulon Press, 2008), 41.

THE SECRET ADMIRER

Dear friends, let us love one another, because love is from God, and everyone who loves has been born of God and knows God.

—1 John 4:7 HCSB

The line crept forward slowly, inch by inch. I craned my neck, scanning the sea of happy, giggling faces for my children.

A smile spread across my own face as I glimpsed my son. Mismatched as usual, he was wearing blue plaid shorts and a red long-sleeved t-shirt. Black ankle socks and sandals completed the look.

I waved as he saw me.

"C'mon, Caitlyn," he yelled, and took off running toward the car.

He clambered in breathlessly, yelling, "I won!" as he buckled his seat belt.

"It's not a contest, Nick," Caitlyn hollered back, grumpy at being second. "Anyway, *last* one in wins!"

I squashed the argument quickly as we made our way out of the circular drive of the elementary school.

Trying to lighten the mood, I asked the typical series of after-school questions: "Did everyone have a good day? What was the best part? Who did you play with at recess?"

Nick piped up first, recounting back the game they played in gym, the song they learned in Spanish, and the ninety he got on his spelling test. My daughter was uncharacteristically silent.

"Honey," I started, glancing in the rearview mirror, "how was *your* day?"

My usually chatty daughter shrugged her shoulders and blushed.

"Caitlyn? Everything okay?"

"I have a secret admirer," she confessed.

"A secret admirer," I exclaimed. "Well, isn't that exciting!"

Actually, I'm not sure if excitement was what I was feeling. A secret admirer? In third grade? Then my thoughts flashed back to the young boy named Tom Williams who'd captured my fancy at age six. I remembered trying to switch seats with another girl so I could sit next to him in class, and the time I deliberately fell playing duck, duck, goose at recess so he'd catch me.

We walked into the house and I began to prepare their snacks.

Caitlyn and Nick pulled their lunch boxes and folders out of their backpacks, handed them to me, and sat down at the kitchen table.

Once snack was over my son ran off to play, but Caitlyn remained at the table. I pulled my chair closer to hers and said, "Tell me about this secret admirer, honey."

She walked over to her folder, pulled out a carefully folded up note, and handed it to me.

Someone had taken a shine to my daughter.

The outside of the note was covered with hearts. The inscription read

from Secret Emierer to Catolan

not from Jakson

My heart swelled and I stifled a grin. I flipped the note over and continued reading.

Secret edmirer

I am sorry you had a bad day today.

By secret enmirerer to Caytlen Carel

Sory I do not know how to spell you name but it is for you.

I asked her if she thought she knew who it was, but she was baffled.

For the rest of the day I watched my daughter walk taller. Was it me, or were her steps a bit lighter and her laugh a bit louder? She had a secret admirer. Of all the girls in the class to admire, this boy picked *her*, and my daughter was radiating the look of one who'd been chosen.

The next day I sat in my study preparing a lesson on the book of Jude. At the start of a Bible study, I always make it a point to talk about the Bible as a whole before diving into a book: What is the Bible and why do we study it? Who is the Bible about? To whom were the specific books or letters written? Why did the author write them and what point was he trying to convey?

As I thought about the last question, my daughter's secret admirer came to mind. This eight-year-old mystery boy had a case of puppy love, and that puppy love was driving him to act.

He wrote the letter because he couldn't not write it.

Do you remember your first crush? Did you write their name on your binder and go out of your way to bump into them in the halls? Did you choose your clothes carefully and take extra time getting ready? Through the years mankind has acted in both heroic courage and horrific folly, all in the name of love. Why?

The same reason the secret admirer (whom I strongly suspected was Jackson) penned his emotions to my daughter.

~ Because love is compelled to express itself ~

The following day another note came home. This time Caitlyn didn't wait for her brother to leave the room to break the news.

"Look, Mommy," she squealed, eyes sparkling with excitement, "I got another note!"

We opened it together and, once again, my heart melted.

Secret Emier!

for Caitlyn Carl. I like you.

The inside of the note offered a clue toward her admirer's identity:

I am close to you But it is not Lucis, Gami, Logan, or Griffin.

By secret Emierer

The admirer, though not ready to fully disclose himself, had begun to make himself known. Why?

~ Because love is compelled to reveal itself ~

The next day my fingers flew across the keyboard as I finished the lesson.

Why did God bother with the Bible? Why did He create the heavens and the earth in first place?

Because God is love, and love is compelled to express itself.

Why did He bother to don a cloak of flesh and step into His creation?

Because God is love, and love is compelled to reveal itself.

The Creator of the Universe longs to reveal Himself to you. Are you tuned to His whispers? Have you created a space for Him in the bustle and busyness of life? Are you seeking Him in the Spirit-inspired, God-breathed words of Scripture?

How do you carry yourself throughout the day? Do you walk with your head bowed and shoulders slouched, or with the purposeful stride of the selected? Is the outpour of your life bitterness and cynicism or sweetness and gratitude?

Friend, before He said, "Let there be light," He knew your name. Before He separated the light from the darkness He'd established your days. Everything you need you have in Him. Every ache in your soul is fulfilled by Him. Every tear you have cried is seen by Him, and every cry of your heart is heard by Him.

It is He who called you and He who perfects you, and though your faith will falter, His love never fails.

Because of His love, He created you.

Because you are His delight, He pursues you.

Because of His grace, He saved you.

Because of His mercy, He forgives you.

Because of His promise, He will glorify you on the last day.

You have captured the heart of your King; walk like one who is chosen.

WATER-SKIS

For since the world began, no ear has heard, and no eye has
seen a God like you, who works for those who wait for Him!

—Isaiah 64:4–NLT

I love big, crazy family vacations. This is a good thing, because I
have a super-sized family with a healthy share of crazy.

One favorite spot is on Grand Lake o' the Cherokees in Jay,
Oklahoma. Mike and I, along with Caitlyn and Nick, my parents, my
two sisters, their two husbands, and their children, rent a house that
sits on the picturesque lake. My sweet grandmother has joined us
twice, putting the total number of bodies in the house at one time at
eighteen.

It's my kind of paradise.

The house is a stone's throw from the marina, so at our disposal are
jet skis, paddle boats, pontoons, tubes, a speedboat, and water-skis.
Once, during a particularly intense season of anxiety, I remembered
the speed boat and what it was like to ski.

I first learned to water-ski in college. I've only done it a handful of
times since, but it's like riding a bike. Once you get the feel for it, you
have it.

I never realized just how counterintuitive the sport was until I tried
to teach some family members how to do it. Everything in you wants
to pull yourself up, but to master the skis the boat must pull you. You
are an active participant in the activity, but it's not your strength you
are skiing in, it's the boat's.

Back to my anxiety. I was thinking about upcoming deadlines and commitments and fighting off the familiar wave of overscheduled-induced-panic.

That morning I had stared at my disheveled image in the bathroom mirror after a poor night's sleep. "I've got a commitment for you," I grumbled. "How about committing yourself?!"

I looked around at my messy bathroom and the counters that needed cleaning. I looked in the closet, riddled with heaps of clothes, then looked up toward the ceiling.

"Are you going to show up?" I asked the Lord. "I can't do this on my own!"

I felt the warmth of the Holy Spirit surround me.

That's right, He whispered, *you can't. So stop trying so hard.* All water-skiers know the pitfall of trying too hard. We want to help the boat, we want to lend our strength, but our efforts land us face down in the lake.

Our job is to prepare; the boat does the rest. Put on the life vest and the water-skis. Jump out of the water and cling to the rope. Put your feet in the proper position and wait. The driver is carefully watching, making sure you are ready and the conditions are right. Then, at the perfect time, he guns the engine. And all you have to do hold on tight and follow the boat.

God has called you for a specific purpose. He has gifted you both spiritually and physically for it. He doesn't need your expertise. He isn't impressed by your resume. There isn't an award, diploma, or accolade that qualifies you to do the work He has prepared for you. God does His mightiest work through willing vessels and obedient hearts. Put on the vest and the water-skis – be prepared. Get your feet in the proper position by studying the Word. Listen carefully for the voice of the Holy Spirit. Cling to Jesus, the source of our salvation. And your Heavenly Father, who watches you carefully every moment, will act at the perfect time.

For I can do everything through Christ, who gives me strength.

—Philippians 4:13

THE CHIA PET

What father among you, if his son asks for a fish, will give
him a snake instead of a fish? Or if he asks for an egg, will
give him a scorpion? If you then, who are evil, know how
to give good gifts to your children, how much more will the
heavenly Father give the Holy Spirit to those who ask Him?

—Luke 11:11–13 HCSB

It had been at least a month since we'd talked, so when my friend's
name popped up on my phone I eagerly answered.

"How are you?" I exclaimed.

Her voice betrayed her exhaustion. It had been a long, difficult few
years, and while they had seen the Lord's hand at work, her heart was
heavy for her son.

We talked for the remainder of my forty-five minute commute
home, and as we hung up, her request was simple.

"Pray for his heart. I think the Lord's got him, but please, pray for
his salvation."

Early the next morning, as I made the long drive from Flower
Mound to downtown Dallas, I did just that. I prayed for her son as
though he were my own, begging the Lord to overwhelm him with
His love, praying that the richness of His grace would be more satisfy-
ing than the distractions of the world.

And as I prayed, I thought of the Chia Pet.

Years ago at a Christmas gift exchange party, I was the amused re-
cipient of a Chia Pet. Actually it was a Chia Herb Garden. My fellow
partygoers howled with laughter as the gift-giver, a friend of mine,
defended her choice.

"These are awesome," she said. "Seriously, I have one and I love it!"

The next day I looked at the package. My black thumb is well-known by those closest to me, and because of that, I shy away from trying to grow things. But then I decided to hold onto it and give it a shot. With the best of intentions, I put the Chia Herb Garden in the pantry on the top shelf and promptly forgot about it.

Fast forward four years.

In a sudden burst of clutter-induced frustration, I attacked the pantry with a vengeance, ruthlessly pulling old mixes and unused cookbooks from the shelves and tossing them into the trash. Old, never-used spices that had sat in a rack gathering dust (what in the world is marjoram, anyway?) and piles of printed-off recipes pre-dating Pinterest were not spared, and neither was anything else that hadn't been used in the past twelve months.

Finally I got to the top shelf.

There, still in its plastic-wrapped box, was the Chia Herb Garden.

"There's no way this is still good," I said to myself as I examined it. But for some reason—curiosity, perhaps, or an urge for fresh oregano—I kept it.

And then I opened it.

And then I followed the directions.

And several weeks later, amazingly, I had an herb garden.

Seeds can sit dormant for a long time. Basil can last up to five years; oregano and sage last four. The innate ability of the seed to grow and produce is not hindered by the lack of ideal conditions; it is simply halted until the conditions are right.

Why should this encourage you today, and what comfort can my friend take from the Chia Pet?

> For just as rain and snow fall from heaven and do not return there without saturating the earth and making it germinate and sprout, and providing seed to sow and food to eat, so My word that comes from My mouth will not return to Me empty, but it will accomplish what I please and will prosper in what I send it to do.
>
> —Isaiah 55:10–11

In both the Old and New Testament the Word of God is likened to a seed. Jesus tells the parable of the sower, in which a farmer goes out to scatter his seed, throwing it without reservation—handful after handful. The seed falls everywhere; on the path, in the thorns, on the rocks, and on good, rich, fertile soil.

Not one area of ground is denied the seed, but only the good soil provides the proper conditions.

The soil represents our hearts. The Farmer's job is to prepare the soil and sow the seed.

The process of preparing the soil can be time consuming: digging, sifting out sand, rocks, and clay; adding organic matter like compost or manure. Finally, when the time is right, the soil is ready for the seed.

As I pray for my friend's son, I pray with confidence. We serve a Heavenly Farmer who cares deeply about the soil of our hearts. He cares enough to allow pain and suffering to do the tedious work of tilling. In fact, He cares far more about the salvation of our loved ones than we could possibly imagine.

My job, my friend's job, and your job, if you are praying for one who looks lost, is to sow the good seed of God's Word, and to pray that the Farmer would tend to the soil.

Had I waited too much longer, the Chia Herb Garden wouldn't have grown. No matter how ripe the conditions may be, basil, oregano, and sage seeds do not last forever. They have a definite and final expiration date.

Not so with God's Word.

Don't ever give up on the one who seems unreachable. Jesus tells us to pray persistently, asking, seeking, and knocking without ceasing, for Gospel-rich seeds of grace have no expiration date.

> Don't be afraid, little flock, because your Father delights to give you the kingdom.
>
> —Luke 12:32

THROW FORGIVE LIKE MO'

Then Peter came to Him and said, "Lord, how many times could my brother sin against me and I forgive him? As many as seven times?"

"I tell you, not as many as seven," Jesus said to him, "but 70 times seven."

—Matthew 18:21–22

What were you doing at age thirteen?

I lived on Churchill Street in Shoreview, Minnesota. My best friends were Jenny Wagner, Molly Benson, Dawn Kuechle, and Nicole Sekeres. I loved Debbie Gibson, Bon Jovi, and Tiffany equally, and I wanted to be a singer.

Dawn had the VHS tape of *Dirty Dancing*, which we watched every time I spent the night at her house. I liked a boy named Leon and rode my bike everywhere I went.

Life was simple.

Life is a little more complicated for a sweet thirteen-year-old girl named Mo'ne Davis.

The young Ms. Davis was thrust into the spotlight at age twelve when she led her baseball team to the Little League World Series, and she was, as *Wikipedia* states, "the first girl to earn a win and pitch a shutout in Little League World Series History."[9]

At thirteen, Davis' fastball was a whopping seventy miles per

---

9 "Mo'ne Davis," *Wikipedia*, http://en.wikipedia.org/wiki/Mo'ne_Davis.

hour—head and shoulders above her age group's average. She excelled at all things athletic, football and basketball included. Perhaps the most notable of her achievements was the cover of the August 2014 issue of *Sports Illustrated*, a first for a Little League player.

All that was nice, but all that was nothing compared to what she did on Monday, March 23, 2015.

First, the big announcement: Disney broke the news that they were making a movie about the baseball star's life called *Throw Like Mo'*.

A college freshman who played baseball at a Pennsylvania University tweeted his displeasure, calling the movie a joke and the thirteen-year-old Mo' a name not worth repeating.

That happened on the evening of Friday, March 20.

By Saturday night, his Twitter account had been deleted and his spot on the college baseball team eliminated. His statement read as follows:

> An example that one stupid tweet can ruin someone's life and I couldn't be more sorry about my actions last night. I please ask you to . . . Forgive me and truly understand that I am in no way shape or form a sexist and I am a huge fan of Mo'ne. She was quite an inspiration.[10]

If this had happened to me at age thirteen (and if you knew my athletic ability, you would be giggling at the impossibility), I would not have forgiven him.

I would have surrounded myself with anyone interested in joining "Team Rebecca." I would have told the story over and over, likely embellishing the details a little bit more with each retelling.

I also would have let this defeat me. While possibly having the wherewithal to hold it together on the outside, this would have wrecked me on the inside.

I wonder if even today I would display the grace that Mo'ne Davis

---

10 Layla A. Jones, "Mo'ne Davis asks Bloomsburg to reinstate player who insulted her," *Philly.com*, March 23, 2015, accessed March 24, 2015, http://www.philly.com/philly/blogs/ trending/Mone-Davis-asks-Bloomsburg-to-reinstate-player-who-insulted-her.html.

gave the young man who surely deserved none.

I hope so.

By Sunday evening, the story had gone viral. Everyone knew of the movie, the tweet, and the university's reaction.

Mo'ne reached out to the president of the school and asked him to reconsider the punishment.

> While I admit I was pretty hurt when I read his comments, I felt sad that he was dismissed from the team. I am sure (name withheld) has worked very hard to get where he is and dreams of playing in the major leagues. For this reason, I'm asking you to please allow him back on the team so that he can continue to chase his dream. He made one dumb mistake. I'm sure he would go back and change it if he could.[11]

Mo'ne Davis behaved in a mature, admirable, Christ-like way. Because of her forgiveness, yes, but she did more than forgive him.

She *interceded* for him.

What the freshman tweeted was awful. Whether or not it was a momentary brain lapse or a glimpse of his true character doesn't matter.

He did not deserve grace. He deserved to be dropped from the team, and Mo'ne, the very object of his scorn, went before the president of his university and pleaded his case.

Whom do you identify with in this story?

I want so much to say Mo'ne.

If I were to be perfectly honest, I would have to say the freshman.

Not because I harbor resentment toward successful young athletes. But if you were to glimpse into my mind for even a moment, you would be shocked. The thoughts that flash through my mind are shameful; thoughts of anger, impatience, jealousy, and scorn. I am not who I want to be nor am I who I appear to be.

How about you? Most of us who have traveled in church circles for a measure of time can walk the walk and talk the talk, but what about

---

11 Ibid.

our motives? What about our secret sin? What about our thoughts? You and I need more than forgiveness and Jesus offers far more.

> Therefore He is able also to save forever those who draw near to God through Him, since He always lives to make intercession for them.
>
> —Hebrews 7:25 NASB

He. Always. Lives. To make intercession. For you.
For me.
When you fail He stands before the Father and pleads your case.
And when you fail again, He does it again.
And again.
And again.
He prays for you. He makes a case for your righteousness. He covers you in His sinlessness because the cross paid for your sinfulness.
Forever.

I don't know Mo'ne's religious background, nor do I know whether or not she fully understood how truly admirable her actions were. But in my mind this bold, brave, beautiful act of grace far outshines anything she could have ever done on the baseball field.

> I pray not only for these, but also for those who believe in Me through their message. May they all be one, as You, Father, are in Me and I am in You. May they also be one in Us, so the world may believe You sent Me.
>
> —John 17:20–21 HCSB

DOORS

And I will forgive their wickedness, and I will never again remember their sins.

—Hebrews 8:12 NLT

If you paid me a nickel every time it happened, I would never need to work again.

With an ear on the news and an eye on the timer, I hurriedly scurried around the kitchen. It was 5:47 p.m., and dinner was supposed to be ready by six so my husband could eat and make it to his small group that met every Tuesday evening at six forty-five.

One glance at the unmade salad and unset table confirmed what I already knew—dinner by six was a pipedream.

Just then, in a simultaneous cacophony, the dog started barking, and the kids started screaming.

Mike was home.

I doubled my speed, striding purposefully to the pantry, and walked through the door to get—

Why in the world did I come in here?

When we purchased our house in 2008, the pantry was a big selling point. It was easily bigger than the walk-in closet in my first apartment. Not huge, mind you, we are a family of modest means, but plenty big enough for me.

With my hands on my hips and a furrowed brow, I scanned the shelves hoping that the sight of something would jog my memory.

No such luck.

I walked back through the door and over to the counter, and as soon as I saw the lettuce, it hit me. Croutons! I turned back to the pantry, grabbed the sealed plastic bag of Texas-sized sourdough salad toppings, and set to work.

Has this ever happened to you? Don't answer. If you are human and your house has doors, it has.

According to University of Notre Dame Psychology Professor Gabriel Radvansky, there is a reason our memories lapse when we move from one room to another. In a research study published in 2011, he coined the term "event boundary."

"Entering or exiting through a doorway serves as an 'event boundary' in the mind, which separates episodes of activity and files them away," he states in *The Quarterly Journal of Experimental Psychology*.[12]

In other words, doorways trigger our inner filing system as we pass through from one room to another. Our minds stop one train of thought, compartmentalize it, and begin a new one. It's like saving a document on your computer, closing it, and starting over. You walk through a door and all of the sudden you are staring at a blank page.

In the Gospel of John, Jesus described Himself as Messiah in seven "I Am" statements.

- 6:35, 48, 51 – "I am the bread of life."

- 8:12 – "I am the light of the world."

- 10:11, 14 – "I am the good shepherd."

- 11:25 – "I am the resurrection and the life."

- 14:6 – "I am the way, the truth, and the life."
- 15:1, 5 – "I am the true vine."

The one that I am most interested in at the moment is found tucked away in chapter 10. If you read too quickly, you'll miss it.

---

12 "Walking through doorways causes forgetting, new research shows," University of Notre Dame, press release, November 18, 2011, accessed June 7, 2016, in *Eurekalert*, http://www.eurekalert.org/pub_releases/2011-11/uond-wtd111811.php.

"I am the door. If anyone enters by Me, he will be saved and
will come in and go out and find pasture."

—John 10:9 HCSB

Scripture tells us that no one comes to the Father unless they come
through Christ, and when that happens, an event boundary of epic
proportions takes place, except we aren't the ones who forget.

God does.

The story of the Old Testament paints a heartbreaking portrait of
the unfaithful Israelites who, in spite of God's rescue from slavery and
deliverance into the land of milk and honey, fall and fail repeatedly.

Idolatry. Drunkenness. Sexual immorality. Failure to take care of
the poor and needy. Forgetting the Sabbath and forsaking the law.

Kind of like us.

Yet no matter how wicked their debauchery gets, God consistently
beckons them back with His offer of mercy.

> But Jacob, you have not called on Me, because, Israel, you
> have become weary of Me.
>
> You have not brought Me your sheep for burnt offerings or
> honored Me with your sacrifices. I have not burdened you
> with offerings or wearied you with incense.
>
> You have not bought Me aromatic cane with silver, or sat-
> isfied Me with the fat of your sacrifices. But you have bur-
> dened Me with your sins; you have wearied Me with your
> iniquities. It is I who sweep away your transgressions for My
> own sake and remember your sins no more.
>
> —Isaiah 43:22–25

So does God have a memory problem?

No, He has a selective memory. In the context of this passage of
Scripture, for God to "remember your sins no more" means He will
not call them to mind and act on them.

When we humbly approach Christ, confessing our belief and re-
penting of that which separates us from Him, we pass from death

to life, from the old to the new, and our sins, as far as our Heavenly Father is concerned, are *gone*.

Locked away in a file that can never be opened. Hurled into the deepest depths of the sea. Scattered as far as the east is from the west. When Christ passed through the door of the tomb, He established a heavenly event boundary that can never be undone.

Because of God's divine forgetfulness, perhaps we can stop punishing ourselves for what has vanished from His sight. Perhaps we, too, can live with the same heavenly memory loss when it comes to those who've offended and hurt us along the way. Not by literally forgetting, but by allowing a holy event boundary to take place; by walking through a metaphorical door and choosing to let the past remain where it is.

> Do not call to mind the former things, or ponder things of the past. Behold, I will do something new, now it will spring forth; will you not be aware of it? I will even make a roadway in the wilderness, rivers in the desert.
>
> —Isaiah 43:18–19 NASB

GIFTS WITH STRINGS

For it is by grace you have been saved, through faith—and
this is not from yourselves, it is the gift of God—

—Ephesians 2:8 NIV

Christmas 2014 was the year we pulled the trigger. I had been so
strong for so long—a mighty oak that could not be toppled—until
years of begging wore me down.

In 2012 my husband suggested it.

"No," I quickly snapped. "They're far too young!"

The following year he hesitatingly tried again.

"Not a chance," I shot back.

In 2014 I changed my mind, mainly because I was tired.

I was tired of the fights, the whining, the begging, the *it's my turn's*
and the *that's not fair's*! I was tired of wiping sticky fingerprints off my
iPad® and I suspected that my sweet husband, who has a much lower
threshold for messy than I do, was tired of the same for his Kindle™.

So in late November I approached Mike with my tail between my
legs and a defeated sigh.

"It's time," I said.

"It is?" he asked.

"It is," I sighed.

Can you guess what the kids found under the tree? It's black and
smooth and rhymes with "spindle."

Christmas of 2014 was the year the kids each got a Kindle™.

Tucking them in on Christmas Eve, I wondered who was more excited, them or me. I remember the feeling as a little girl, lying awake for

hours, ears straining to hear the sound of hooves on rooftops, desperately hoping I'd been good enough to warrant Santa's favor. My eyes always popped open long before the house was awake. I would carefully extract myself from bed, tiptoe down the hall, avoid the creaky stair, and then gaze in wonderment at the piles of presents under the tree.

Although part of me was wary of giving them a tablet, another part could scarcely wait to see them tear off the paper and squeal with delight.

On Christmas morning they did just that.

"Mo-om," my daughter screamed, drawing an extra syllable out of a one-syllable word, "Mo-om! You said you weren't gonna get us one! You said not til we were ten!"

What can I say? I'm weak.

My son nearly barreled me over with his full-body bear hug.

"Worth it," I silently mouthed to my beaming husband.

They tore through the rest of the gifts quickly. I refilled my coffee, started the cinnamon rolls, and smiled, watching Mike set up their tablets.

Then came the strings.

"Okay you two, sit down," my husband said in his best you're-not-in-trouble-but-I-mean-business voice. "We have some rules to establish."

"Number one," I said, "we are going to let you play on them as much as you want today. But after today, thirty minutes a day, just like when you play with mine or Daddy's."

"Mo-om," Caitlyn whined.

I quickly cut her off.

"Number two. You have to maintain a B average in school. If you can't keep your grades up, they go back to us until the next report card."

At this Caitlyn smirked. "I have an A average," she stated proudly.

"Yes, you do," I replied, "and I'm very proud of you.

"Number three," I continued, "your Kindle™ never goes in your bedroom with the door shut. You play with it in the living room or the study where we can see you."

Mike and I went over the rest of the rules, explaining each of them as we went: all devices charge overnight in our bedroom, extra time earned for good behavior, and on and on.

Later, once the house had quieted down, I thought about the many strings attached to their presents.

The tablets were a free gift to my children. They had done nothing to earn them; they had spent nothing on them. Had my husband and I added up all of their good deeds and all of their mischief, I fear mischief might have won. No, the Kindle™ had not been earned. But Mike and I love our children, wanted to do something to delight them, and chose to set our favor upon them.

The gift in and of itself was free. Keeping it, however, was not.

We make a grave error when we live as though God gives as we do.

> This righteousness is given through faith in Jesus Christ to all who believe. There is no difference between Jew and Gentile, for all have sinned and fall short of the glory of God, and all are justified freely by his grace through the redemption that came by Christ Jesus.
>
> —Romans 3:22–24

Did you skip over the Scripture? Go back and read it. Now read it again, slowly. Savor every sentence and digest every word. Say it out loud and own it, because your peace of mind just might hinge on this: Your salvation was free.

It was free. You did not deserve it. God did not look upon you, weigh your good deeds against the bad, and deem you worthy. Think about the state you were in when He saved you. The Bible doesn't say you were bad, good, getting better, or great; the Bible says you were dead.

> As for you, you were dead in your transgressions and sins . . .
>
> —Ephesians 2:1

Last time I checked, dead people don't do much.

Now before you get depressed, think about the implications here. If you did nothing to earn the favor of God, then you can't lose it, either.

I have to say it again because it's huge. Since you did nothing to earn the favor of God, there is nothing you can do to lose it. This means you can stop.

You can step off the spiritual treadmill and rest. Nothing exhausts the Christ-follower more than trying to be good enough. You're not good enough, and neither am I. Neither is anybody else.

As it is written: "There is no one righteous, not even one."

—Romans 3:10

You can stop trying to do more or be more. You could never do enough to earn your salvation, never be good enough to make it on your own merit. As one of my favorite pastors likes to say, "The only thing we bring to our salvation is the sin that makes it necessary."

It didn't take long after receiving their tablets that Caitlyn and Nick got in trouble for fighting and had them taken away. You see, while the Kindle™ was given to them freely, they had to work to keep it.

How many times have you or I felt compelled to continue earning the salvation that was freely given to us?

There are no strings on God's grace. His grace is promiscuous, lavishing the adulteress, the thief, and the tax collector with a love that won't let go. It snakes its way into the deepest, darkest pits and extracts the heinous, the outcast, and the uttermost dregs of society. His grace is completely and utterly unfair.

The grace of God pays the hard worker and the latecomer the same wages. It shares bread with those who betray Him and drinks wine with the one who denies Him. It gives the fattened calf to the prodigal and forsakes the ninety-nine to bring back the one.

God's grace knows no bounds.

It is God's grace that saved you. Not your past. Not your potential. Not your pedigree.

You can stop sucking in your sin and trying to impress. You can slowly exhale and rest.

Not rest on your laurels, though. Does the grace of God free you up to screw things up? No. And if that is the attitude one takes, then they haven't tasted grace.

When we come face-to-face with who we are—not who people think we are but who we really are—when we come face-to-face with the reality of our depravity, and the beautiful truth that God saved us anyway, we will be freed up to joyfully serve Him who freed us.

He was perfectly sinless. We are perfectly sinful. We deserve the worst. He stepped off the throne into flesh and took the punishment for our crimes. He stands between our accuser and the Father.

He takes our worst and exchanges it with righteousness, perfection, and salvation. No strings. No tricks. No games.

Only the promise of forever in the presence of our Savior.

> But because of his great love for us, God, who is rich in mercy, made us alive with Christ even when we were dead in transgressions—it is by grace you have been saved. And God raised us up with Christ and seated us with him in the heavenly realms in Christ Jesus, in order that in the coming ages he might show the incomparable riches of his grace, expressed in his kindness to us in Christ Jesus. For it is by grace you have been saved, through faith—and this is not from yourselves, it is the gift of God—not by works, so that no one can boast. For we are God's handiwork, created in Christ Jesus to do good works, which God prepared in advance for us to do.
>
> —Ephesians 2:4–10

iPad® is a registered trademark of Apple, Inc.
Kindle™ is a trademark of Amazon.com, Inc. or its affiliates.

BELOW SOUND

The LORD confides in those who fear him; he makes his covenant known to them.

—Psalm 25:14

It was a last minute, scarcely planned trip to Florida. My aunt and uncle were driving upstate and my grandmother, who lived in an apartment adjacent to their house, couldn't be left alone. My mother was supposed to go, but my father had just finished radiation for throat cancer, and as if that weren't enough, they were selling their house.

"I could go," I offered.

That was all it took. Two phone calls later (one to my husband and one to my grandma), the ticket was purchased and the plans were set. I would fly to Florida, stay four days while my uncle and his family went to a wedding, and fly back the same day they came home.

"Grandma is very weak," said Uncle Bruce. "She thinks she can do far more than she can, so she's going to try to make a lot of plans. Don't let her."

Knowing my grandma, I smiled. There was no talking her out of something once her mind was made up.

"Try not to let her cook," he continued. "When she stands for too long, she's sore the next day."

I was looking forward to the visit. Grandma was ninety-seven years old, which made every moment precious. I also had a lot of studying and writing to do, so a quiet house in Fort Lauderdale held a lot of appeal.

The day I arrived she was waiting outside. My heart swelled in my chest and a lump rose in my throat. She used a walker now, and arthritis had twisted and bent the fingers that had baked apple pies, sewn dresses, and built dollhouses for as long as I could remember.

Her spirit, however, was as young as always.

She laughed as she gave me a hug and we went inside.

My uncle was right—Grandma had more plans than energy, so most of our time was spent in her little apartment reminiscing.

One story, in particular, gripped me and hasn't let go.

> He reveals the deep and hidden things; He knows what is in the darkness, and light dwells with Him.
>
> —Daniel 2:22 HCSB

It was the story of Mammoth Cave.

When my grandparents were younger, they took my mom and her brother (Uncle Bruce) to central Kentucky to visit Mammoth Cave National Park. The cave system is the largest in the world, with approximately 400 miles of surveyed passageways[13] and descending to a depth of nearly 380 feet.[14]

The tours range in length from one to six hours, geared toward both the first-timers and the crazy off-roaders wanting to belly crawl and squeeze their way through the path less traveled.

Grandma described the trek. Hours spent walking downhill, twisting and turning with no sense of time or direction. Then the tour guide told them to stop and turn off their lamps.

With the soft hand of her son in one hand and her lantern in the other, she did as the tour guide asked.

One by one, the lights went out and a hush fell over the group.

The darkness was tangible, palpable. It was thick and black and un-

---

13 "Mammoth Cave National Park," *Wikipedia*, accessed January 18, 2016, https://en.wikipedia.org/wiki/Mammoth_Cave_National_Park.
14 "Did You Know that Kentucky is the Home of the World's Longest Cave?" University of Kentucky, accessed January18, 2016, https://www.uky.edu/KGS/education/mammothcave.htm.

relenting; pressing in on every side until my grandmother thought she would scream.

"Okay, everyone. You're doing great. I'm going to illustrate to you just how far below the earth we are and then we'll turn on our lights."

At that, he dropped a match.

"You wouldn't believe the sound of that match," Grandma exclaimed, "like it was right next to my ear. It just about filled the whole room."

I laughed, shaking my head, not really wanting to experience it for myself.

"We were below sound, you know," she continued. "The tour guide said that at that depth, almost three-hundred feet down, we were completely below sound. Nothing on the surface could reach us."

Imagine it: being so silent and still, so distraction free, that a match falling to the ground sounds like the clanging of a gong.

When was the last time you went *below sound* with God?

What would your life look like if you made a regular appointment with the Lord to be so quiet, so still, so free from the white noise of society, that His whisper was unmistakable?

Proverbs 3:32 says "the LORD detests the perverse but takes the upright into his confidence." Linger on that for a moment. Let it marinate before you move on.

The King of Heaven and Earth wants to confide in you.

The God of the Universe has things He wants to say to you. They are the deep things, the hidden things; the things only you would understand. He won't tell them to your pastor and He won't say it to me, because they are for you, and He wants to tell you Himself.

Throughout the course of my years in ministry I can tell you this with certainty: The most powerful moments with God have always been in quiet intimacy. Not at worship concerts and not at conferences. Not through Beth Moore and not from Billy Graham. Just me and Him; candle lit, Bible open, and a heart ready to receive.

As you tour the Gospels and trace Jesus' steps, you will notice a pattern. After hours and days spent ministering, Jesus would slip away to a lonely place.

To rest.

To pray.

To listen.

To receive.

You and I have that same invitation, an invitation to an audience with the King. An invitation to hear from God. To go deeper—deeper in the Word and in your knowledge of Him. Below sound and beyond distractions, where the soft whisper of the Spirit is unmistakable and the healer of all things collides with your deepest hurt.

The invitation is always present and never revoked, for the LORD longs to minister to you.

My prayer is that you would say "yes."

> My heart has heard you say, "Come and talk with me." And my heart responds, "LORD, I am coming."
>
> —Psalm 27:8 NLT

SKELETONS

Be on guard, so that your hearts will not be weighted down with dissipation and drunkenness and the worries of life, and that day will not come on you suddenly like a trap . . .

—Luke 21:34 NASB

Hi. I'm Rebecca, and I'm an alcoholic.

It took me a long time to be able to say or write that without squirming on the inside and wishing I could disappear. Now I can say it all day long without flinching.

Hi. I'm Rebecca, and I'm an alcoholic.

I never put vodka in my coffee and I didn't drink every day. I didn't get drunk every time I drank, but I am an alcoholic nonetheless.

Alcoholics do dumb things, reckless things.

Like the time I drank too much on a girls' trip and fell out of a tree.

Or the time I woke up in a different city.

Or the time I got pulled over for drinking and driving the night before my youngest sister's wedding.

Or . . .

Or . . .

Or . . .

For years those skeletons hung neatly in the back of my closet, organized according to shock value, each skeleton worse than the one before, each hidden with utmost care. I still haven't told you the worst of them.

Like the time I drove with my six-week-old baby in the car after three margaritas and half a bottle of wine.

Yes, I did that.

As I type those words—those particular words—I realize that skeleton-sharing can come with a price. Opening the closet door is risky. After all, I co-host a morning show on a Christian radio station. I teach the Bible and speak at Christian Women's Conferences.

My past could disqualify me for that. You might not listen to my show. You might not read my book or my blog.

You might not like me.

That's the scary one, right there. You see, not only am I, by God's grace, a recovered alcoholic, I am a recovering people-pleaser. I am in approval detoxification as I type. So bringing the skeletons out into the light could very easily shatter the image I have worked so carefully to create.

But they could also set you free, and so I will let you in.

I threw the door wide open not long ago. Can I tell you about it? It gives purpose to my murky past.

> But if we are afflicted, it is for your comfort and salvation; or
> if we are comforted, it is for your comfort, which is effective
> in the patient enduring of the same sufferings which we also
> suffer . . .
>
> —2 Corinthians 1:6

We had never met before. In a desperate attempt to help, her husband reached out via e-mail.

He had heard me share my story on-air and wondered if I could talk to his wife.

Tears streamed from her eyes as she struggled to get the words out. Her drinking was out of control and she didn't know what to do. Several stays in rehab and a twelve-step recovery program had not slowed her down.

One day she cried out to God. Then she cried out to her husband.

When we met she was twenty-eight days sober.

As she shared, I discovered something. It wasn't the drinking that paralyzed her.

It was the shame.

She had skeletons, too. Years and years of bad decisions. Closet after closet full of shameful secrets, carefully hidden away.

Here is a glimpse into the mind of a drunk: You drink to drown the pain. The drinking causes more pain. More pain leads to more drinking and on and on the cycle goes.

So I opened my closet to share my skeletons, except there were no skeletons to be found.

Light has a way of breaking down old bones and the Lord has shined His light into the darkest recesses of my soul. The skeletons are gone and only the stories are left.

Stories of how God took a broken girl with her broken life and bandaged her up and set her heart free.

Stories of a merciful God wiping the tear-stained eyes of His daughter who was desperately trying to find her way.

Stories of a patient God gently guiding His lost and wayward child back to the path of life.

Stories of a mighty God who takes our deepest shame and turns it into a deadly weapon pointed straight at the enemy's camp.

Would you believe, as I held her hands and prayed out loud in the coffee shop, that I was oh so thankful for my sin-stained past?

Would you believe, sitting where I sit and knowing what I know, that if I could go back and choose a different story I would stick with the one I've got (minus the drinking and driving, of course)?

That is no small thing. I have known despair. I have struggled with suicidal thoughts. I have longed to end my life.

But as I observed the way my story brought hope to her broken heart, this is what I told the Lord:

"Thank you, God, for allowing me to endure what I've endured. Thank you for giving me a ministry of empathy for those who desperately need to talk to one who's been there."

Sometimes we need someone who can tell us what to do.

Sometimes we need someone who has been there, done that, and lived.

Friend, what skeletons hang in your closet? What sin has stained your soul? There is nothing you've done that the light of Christ can't heal. There is no pain that He can't repurpose and no transgression He can't repair.

Your past is not too dark. Your mistakes are not too many, for His mercies never run dry.

Your shame in the hands of the enemy is a weapon of mass emotional destruction—a nuclear explosion waiting to happen.

But your deepest shame, placed in the hands of your loving Father, just might be the very thing that sets the captives free.

Praise you, Father, for turning skeletons that shame into stories that heal and for making dry bones dance.

> This is what the Sovereign Lord says to these bones: "I will make breath enter you, and you will come to life. I will attach tendons to you and make flesh come upon you and cover you with skin; I will put breath in you, and you will come to life. Then you will know that I am the Lord." So I prophesied as I was commanded. And as I was prophesying, there was a noise, a rattling sound, and the bones came together, bone to bone.
>
> —Ezekiel 37:5–7 NIV

A BIRD IN THE HAND

I know, LORD, that Your judgments are just and that You
have afflicted me fairly.

—Psalm 119:75 HCSB

We stood awkwardly on the doorstep; my husband holding the
door, the babysitter avoiding our eyes and insisting everything was
okay, and me, apologizing for the behavior of one of my children.

Mike and I had enjoyed a rare dinner out with friends and hired
Audrey, one of the children's favorite sitters.

As our evening drew to a close, I realized that I had never glanced
at my phone—not even once. Typically I kept it close at hand just in
case something went wrong.

In nearly nine years of motherhood, nothing ever had.

Until that night.

"Oh no," I said, causing everyone to turn.

"Honey, everything okay?" my husband asked.

"Well, it is now," I said, skimming through several text messages,
"but Audrey was having a tough time, and I missed her call."

We said goodbye to our friends and drove the three blocks to our
house.

Audrey filled me in as I walked her out.

Oh mercy, I thought to myself, *she's never going to come back.*

And that brings us to the doorstep.

It was January and the temperature was below freezing. Mike wanted to shut the door, Audrey wanted to go home, but in true Rebecca
form, I continued with the apologies.

That's when it happened.

Something big and black streaked past us and into the house, moving so quickly that none of us were certain it had happened.

"Did you see that?"

"What *was* that?"

"If that was a bat, I'm moving!"

"Caitlyn," I called out, but before I could finish, she cried, "Mommy! There's a bird in the house! A bird just flew in the house!"

Darting back and forth, the poor bird was clearly terrified. What had looked promising from the outside was instead a small, enclosed space with shouting, commotion, and a six-foot man chasing it with a broom.

We developed a plan and set it in motion: Caitlyn holding the front door open, me at the back, and Audrey and Nick trying to help Mike move the terrified bird toward an exit.

Another black streak, and this time it was my son hollering.

"Mom! Dad! The bird went upstairs! I think it's in my room!"

I raced up the steps two at a time and began closing all the bedroom doors, hoping to keep it in one spot. Finally, with the bird trapped in Nick's room, we all looked at each other.

"Now what do we do?" asked Caitlyn.

Mike firmly took control. Gripping the broom, he strode purposefully into my son's room and closed the door.

Several minutes later he emerged, holding a thrashing, checkered pillowcase tightly in one hand.

"Did you kill it?" I asked without thinking.

"Does it look like its dead?" he shot back.

We all followed my husband as he stepped into the front yard and gingerly set the pillowcase on the ground. Pulling it open, he nudged the bird out and watched as it flew off.

You and I are just like the bird.

> May Your compassion come to me so that I may live, for
> Your instruction is my delight.
>
> —Psalm 119:77

That poor bird was so limited in its understanding. It had seen a light and flown toward it. The light and the warmth seemed right. But once it was in the house, what first appeared as a sanctuary was loud and small and frightening—not at all a pleasant place to be.

The bird had no way of knowing that the big man with the broom wanted to help. The bird only knew that someone was swinging something big at it.

When my husband was finally able to corner the bird, it was nearly paralyzed with fear. It didn't understand his words, so Mike was unable to make the bird see that if it would just put its trust in him, he would set it free.

From the bird's perspective, the world was spinning out of control.

My husband is bigger, stronger, and wiser than the bird. He knows things that the bird can't in its limited understanding. The bird couldn't see the way out, but Mike could. And Mike, being a gentle and loving man, put the bird in a small space and a dark place for a brief period of time, all the while knowing that what he was doing was kind.

Mike acted in love. And what seemed like the worst thing for the bird was the very key to its freedom.

Sometimes life goes well.

Most of the time life just goes.

But sometimes it seems as though the walls are caving in and the ground is shaking. Sometimes our circumstances seem to trap us in a dark place with no space.

The one you call your Heavenly Father is sovereign over the entire universe. There is not a place so vast He doesn't fill it nor a space so microscopic He can't see it. And that means that nothing comes to you without His permission. Everything that reaches you has passed through your Father's hands. And Scripture promises that God works all things for the good of those who love Him, no matter how earth-shattering our circumstances are.

Literally.

My co-host, Jeff Taylor, and I interviewed author Kariss Lynch on 90.9 KCBI about her novel *Shaken*. Kariss got the idea for the book the day the earthquake hit Haiti in 2010. The heroine of the story, a missionary, lives through the quake and struggles to understand how God could allow such a horrible disaster on such an impoverished people.

Kariss had visited the island two years after the fact, and I asked her if she had reconciled that question for herself. Her answer was as profound as it was concise:

> The most interesting thing I saw as we went from village to village was the impact that the evangelists had on the Haitians. People say before the earthquake it was 80 percent Catholic, 20 percent Protestant, and 100 percent voodoo. But after the earthquake American missionaries starting showing up by the hundreds and many of the Haitians began following what they call, 'The best way.' They're following Jesus. So yes, God is always working, even when the ground is shaking.

> God is always working.

> Even when the ground is shaking.

You and I simply cannot see life from the Lord's perspective, but we can understand His perspective better through His Word.

You have been chosen and called. He has a purpose for you that *only you* can fulfill, and only by trusting Him. You and I need refining, and it is through trials that we are refined. And as a goldsmith holds his precious metal to the fire, being ever so careful to pull it at just the right time, so your Heavenly Father holds you.

The poor bird will probably never fly this way again. It has no way of understanding the act of love that was extended to it, but you and I are different.

God's act of love toward you was made perfect in the Body of Christ as He extended His arms on the cross. So the next time you feel the ground shaking and the walls caving in remember these truths: Your Father is sovereign over all. Nothing gets to you without passing through His hands. If He allows it, you can be sure He will bring beauty out of it.

> I am weary from grief;
> strengthen me through Your word.
> Keep me from the way of deceit

and graciously give me Your instruction.
I have chosen the way of truth;
I have set Your ordinances before me.
I cling to Your decrees;
Lord, do not put me to shame.
I pursue the way of Your commands,
for You broaden my understanding.

—Psalm 119:28–32

DRIVING IN RAIN

You discern my going out and my lying down; you are familiar with all my ways. Before a word is on my tongue you, LORD, know it completely. You hem me in behind and before, and you lay your hand upon me.

—Psalm 139:3–5 NLT

When was the last time you drove in rain? And I don't mean a light mist or soft drizzle; I mean *rain*.

April 2015 was the April of rain in the Dallas/Fort Worth area. I don't know exactly how many inches we got, but it was enough to rain out over half of my two children's softball and baseball games.

April was also the month that my radio station, 90.9 KCBI, took a week to deviate from regular programming. Because the KCBI radio network is non-commercial, we have to find financial support from other sources. The "other sources" are our generous listeners.

I never mind the fundraising, which is strange, considering that I can scarcely ask someone for a favor, let alone money. But I believe passionately in both the message and the ministry of the radio station, so when the time rolls around, I roll up my sleeves and ask.

This time, however, I started the week more than a little nervous as to how I was going to make it through to the end. April was, by far, my busiest month of the year. I had spent the previous two weekends leading back-to-back retreats, and sandwiched in between was a flurry of evening kid-related activities; difficult for a mom who sets her alarm for 3:15 a.m. During the fundraiser, Jeff Taylor and I work both the morning and afternoon shifts, which means five consecutive nights away from our families. My daughter's birthday happened to fall that week, so on Wednesday night my family celebrated nine years of Caitlyn without me.

Thursday morning I crawled out of bed as one waking from a coma: groggy, confused, and exhausted to the point of collapse. It was raining—make that *pouring*—and my white-knuckled grip on the wheel as I drove to our downtown Dallas office was making my fingers numb.

Suddenly my mind flashed back to another storm, this one from my childhood. My sisters and I sat nestled in the backseat of the family Buick. Dad was behind the wheel and Mom was nervous. As lightening flashed and thunder roared, as rain angrily pelted the window, I closed my eyes, pulled my blanket up around my neck and surrendered peacefully to sleep.

I felt completely secure.

Why? How?

Because my dad was behind the wheel. And because I trusted my dad, neither the lightening, the thunder, nor the rain frightened me.

After the morning shift I called my father to confirm whether or not that was an actual memory.

"I certainly do remember that storm," he said. "We were coming back from your grandfather's funeral. But it wasn't rain, it was ice. A thunder-ice storm—I'd never seen anything like it. And your mother was terrified. But there was an 18-wheeler in front of me, and I was able to drive in the ruts he made on the snow. As long as I stayed in the ruts there was no way I could slide off the road."

Did you catch that?

My father drove into the unknown with confidence, because someone bigger and more powerful had gone before him to pave the way, and I, just ten years old, slept, fully trusting my dad to get us safely through to the other side.

April 2015 had brought more than stormy conditions to North Texas; it had ushered in a few personal storms of my own. Later that day, my Heavenly Father showed me that, just like the 18-wheeler that had gone before my dad, so He went before me, straightening my path and clearing the way so I could boldly move forward in faith.

Are *you* in a storm?

My friend, you can loosen your white-knuckled grip on the wheel.

Your Heavenly Father has paved the way for you. He goes before you, stays by your side, and follows behind.

He hems you in.

You can exhale and relax into His arms, because He is driving you through the wind and rain, and He will see you safely through to the other side.

You are so secure in Him.

By Friday afternoon, the rain had stopped and small pockets of blue began to spread across the sky. Before making the drive back to the office for the final leg of our fundraiser, I sat by the window with my Bible open to Matthew, chapter eight.

> When He got into the boat, His disciples followed Him. And behold, there arose a great storm on the sea, so that the boat was being covered with the waves; but Jesus Himself was asleep. And they came to Him and woke Him, saying, "Save us, Lord; we are perishing!" He said to them, "Why are you afraid, you men of little faith?" Then He got up and rebuked the winds and the sea, and it became perfectly calm. The men were amazed, and said, "What kind of a man is this, that even the winds and the sea obey Him?"
>
> —Matthew 8:23–27 NASB

This is what I know and this is what I cling to when the winds howl and the waves rise: He may not always calm the sea. Sometimes the storms of life rage on no matter how hard we pray. But when I come to Jesus in His Word, seeking Him for who He is and not what He can do, I remember that the disciples learned priceless lessons in the midst of the most fearsome storms. I remember that the fingers that spread out the expanse of the stars still hold me in their grip. He still counts the hairs on our heads and knows every sparrow that falls from the sky.

Yes, while He may not calm the sea, He can calm the storm in me.

And in you.

And in all who come to believe.

THE RING

My husband grew up spending his summers on the sunny shores of Port Aransas, Texas.

Every summer for the past six years, our small family of four makes the eight hour trip from the Dallas/Fort Worth area to spend a week digging our toes into that same sand.

It is my kind of paradise.

The town is small and old, but charming. The atmosphere is laid back and relaxed. The beaches are clean, the seafood is fresh, and our little tribe has fun together.

Each year, Mike and I allot the children a certain amount of vacation money. The money is theirs to spend as they wish, but once it's gone, it's gone—a lesson hard learned by my daughter the first year. Her crisp twenty-dollar bill was left at the first truck stop we walked into in exchange for a fake porcelain doll and an armful of candy.

Since then, the kids have learned to hang onto their cash at least until we make it to the coast.

The tiny town on Mustang Island is no stranger to visitors, boasting street after street of your typical touristy souvenir shops. You know the kind—aisles of tie-dyed T-shirts, corny mugs, and tacky trinkets laden with silly slogans like "Port-A All the Way!"

Seriously, people pay for that stuff, and too much, at that.

Count my son among the suckers.

I don't know the name of the store. All I can tell you is that it's neon orange with a bright blue sign running the length of the building that screams, "All bathing suits $9.99! All brand-name clothing half off!"

You have to watch your step when you walk in, as the store seems to sit about twelve inches off the ground. It's dark and dank with a low ceiling, ill-suited for those of us with claustrophobic tendencies. I'd been there five minutes when I'd had enough, but Nick was taking his time.

He slowly made his way from one aisle to the next, carefully examining and picking up various items of different shapes and sizes.

"Come on, buddy," I called out after a few more minutes had passed. My husband looked at me and sharply shook his head. Shrugging my shoulders, I walked off to find our daughter.

Caitlyn hadn't found anything either, so the two of us decided to make our way across the parking lot to another store, one that had a giant great white shark head for a door.

About ten minutes later, Mike and Nick walked in. Nick was absolutely beaming.

"Mom," he cried, running in my direction, "Look what I got, Mom!"

His small hand was clenched into a tight fist. He opened his hand and pressed something hard and sweaty into my palm.

It was a ring.

A mood ring with tiny @ symbols on it, each spaced about five millimeters apart.

"It's for you, Mom."

I looked at the ring and looked at my son.

"Did you buy this, Nick?"

"Yep! With my own money," he said, eyes shining with pride. "Do you like it?"

"Oh, buddy," I said softly, forcing the words around the lump in my throat, "I love it more than anything. I'm going to wear it all the time."

Satisfied, Nick ran off to find his sister.

"Did you give him extra money for that?" I asked, turning to my husband.

"No," said Mike. "He wanted to buy you a present. He told me that before we got there."

"Did he buy himself anything?" I pressed, wanting more details.

"A few little things. Nothing big. He wanted to make sure he could afford your ring."

I was undone.

Completely, totally, and utterly undone.

You know what it is about that gift that turns me into a melted pile of mommy-mush?

(Hint: It's not the ring, although I wear it all the time.)

It's the cost. You see, in a simple act of love, my son had sacrificed a sizable chunk of his prized vacation money to adorn my finger with a mood ring decorated with @ symbols.

When you truly love someone, you are willing to sacrifice.

My son has bought me little things before, and has sometimes used money that he's saved up from an odd job here or a little chore there. Usually when he does, it's only a matter of time before the strings show up.

"Can I have some candy, Mom?"

"No, honey, you don't need any candy."

"Even though I got you that _____?"

This time it was different. No strings, no take backs, and no guilt trips when he ran out of money and couldn't buy a boogie board. Just a beautiful, precious, priceless gift that my son wanted me to have.

When I look at the ring, I think of the sacrifice my son made, and I can't help but think of another sacrifice.

One that was made for you. One that is more priceless and more precious than a million rings made from the rarest of gems.

> For God so loved the world, that He gave His only begotten Son, that whoever believes in Him shall not perish, but have eternal life. For God did not send the Son into the world to judge the world, but that the world might be saved through Him.
>
> —John 3:13–17

When God created the world, it was perfect. When sin entered in through the fateful bite of a forbidden fruit, everything that was good and beautiful became fractured and broken, and mankind was separated from the Creator.

The price tag of sin reads "death," and there are no discounts.

Do you remember what Jesus said on the cross?

Therefore when Jesus had received the sour wine, He said, "It is finished!" And He bowed His head and gave up His spirit.

—John 19:30

"It is finished." The Greek word at play here is an old accounting word: *tetelestai.*

It means finished, completed, consummated—*paid in full.*

When Jesus sacrificed Himself on the cross He paid our debt—yours and mine—in full.

We are sinners. Sin has a price. The price is death. Because God is holy and just, the price must be paid. Jesus paid with His life so that you and I may live.

Why?

One word.

Love.

Because when you truly love someone, no cost is too high and no sacrifice too great.

My son found me worthy of his vacation money, and I have a precious ring as a reminder.

Your Lord finds you worthy of His Son, and did not hesitate to send Him to the cross so that you might be gathered into His arms.

May you receive His gift and bask forever in the love of your Savior.

DEAR BRIDGETTE

But as for me, the nearness of God is my good; I have made the Lord GOD my refuge, that I may tell of all Your works.

—Psalm 73:28

It was late, and I was tired. When your alarm goes off as early as mine, seven-thirty in the evening feels like midnight.

The dishes were cleaned and put away, thanks to an extremely helpful hubby. One kid was in the tub, and the other was working on math. I went to power down my computer and put it in the car—my final step before heading upstairs to bed—and that's when I saw the e-mail.

It shouted at me, urgently demanding my attention, with "FEELING LOST" spelled out in all caps across the subject line.

Don't do it, I thought to myself.

You know better than to open e-mail right before bed, I insisted.

You can do it tomorrow, I pleaded.

I didn't listen.

I opened the e-mail and sat down. My eyes flicked across the screen, scanning quickly at first then slowing down to absorb what I'd read.

We'll call her Bridgette, and Bridgette's story broke my heart.

She had not grown up knowing the Lord. In fact, she had run as far from Him as she possibly could. The bad choices and left turns added up until one day, at the end of her rope, she cried out.

"I didn't pray for salvation," she wrote, "I prayed for one single moment of joy."

The Lord did give her joy, and salvation, too.

He also gave her a wonderful husband and a beautiful son.

In 2004, in Bridgette's words, "He took my son home."
But there was more:

> My life is so scattered . . . and I cannot seem to get back
> where I once was in Him . . . PLEASE PRAY . . . GIVE ME
> SOME ADVISE [sic]. I listen [to KCBI] all day every day.
> I love the ministering/music . . . but I still feel so far away
> from Him, and I only want to be at His feet . . . HELP!!!

Have you ever felt this way? Alone in your pain and your grief? Has the knowledge in your head stubbornly refused to make its way down to your heart?

You are not alone.

I sat down and wrote Bridgette back, fingers flying over the keyboard as fast as I could think. I loved on her, expressed my deepest sorrow over the loss of her son, and promised to pray for her. I thanked her for listening to KCBI and trusting me with her heart. Then I asked her a question.

"Are you spending any time with God in His Word?"

You see, music and teaching are good tools, but they are no substitute for quiet time with the Lord. Just you and Him; Bible open, pen and paper ready, with heart and mind willing to receive.

I say this often both on the air and when I speak: You can't ride the coattails of someone else's faith when the day of trouble comes.

I love good teaching. I sit under plenty of it. I take other people's Bible studies and read other authors' books, but if that is all I ever do then my relationship with Jesus is a vicarious one, and a vicarious relationship is not a relationship, it's an observation.

David had a relationship with the Lord.

He called God *YAHWEH Raah*, "The Lord is my Shepherd."

David knew firsthand God's provision and protection. He also knew this:

> "The LORD confides in those who fear him; he makes his
> covenant known to them."
>
> —Psalm 25:14 NIV

Solomon, David's son, knew it too:

"For the LORD detests the perverse but takes the upright into his confidence."

—Proverbs 3:32

Did you catch it?

God wants to confide in you.

That might be the most important thing you digest all day.

The Creator of the Universe, He who sits enthroned above the circle of the earth, the One who exists outside of time and space yet occupies all time and space wants to confide in you.

In *you.*

The Lord has things He wants to tell you that He is not going to tell me.

Because they're for you.

He has things to say to you that He won't say to your pastor.

He's waiting on you.

No one knows your heart like He does. No one knows your hurts like He does. No one knows your headaches, your habits, your hangups like He does.

No one can minister to you as He can, but His primary means of ministry is through His Word, the Bible.

I won't reprint Bridgette's entire letter, but one thing she wrote concerned me. She was waiting for a feeling. She wanted an experience. She needed the goosebumps-chills-shivers-mountaintop moment to feel close to God.

Sometimes I get that, and it's awesome.

But most of the time when I experience Him, I'm experiencing Him through His Word.

Please hear me when I say this in love: there is no knowing Him outside of His Word. There is no experiencing Him apart from that which agrees with His Word. There is no growing in Him unless you are rooted in His Word.

There is *no relationship* with Him outside of His Word.

Jesus made this abundantly clear to His disciples on the night before He went to the cross.

I am the true vine, and My Father is the vinedresser. Every

branch in Me that does not bear fruit, He takes away; and every branch that bears fruit, He prunes it so that it may bear more fruit. You are already clean because of the word which I have spoken to you.

—John 15:1–3 NASB; emphasis mine

Jesus draws near to us through His Word.

Abide in Me, and I in you. As the branch cannot bear fruit of itself unless it abides in the vine, so neither can you unless you abide in Me.

—John 15:4

As we abide in His Word through faithful study, Jesus empowers us to walk out our Father's will for our lives through obedience to His Word.

Just as the Father has loved Me, I have also loved you; abide in My love. If you keep My commandments, you will abide in My love; just as I have kept My Father's commandments and abide in His love.

—John 15:9 –10

To abide in His Word is to abide in His perfect love, and perfect love casts out fear and replaces it with joy.

These things I have spoken to you so that My joy may be in you, and that your joy may be made full.

—John 15:11

Bridgette told me in a later e-mail that she had never really read the Bible on any consistent basis. She had reached out to her favorite radio station because she felt lost, hopeless, and all alone.

That is how she *felt*.

I don't want to diminish her feelings. Her feelings were real, and her feelings were important, but her feelings were not lining up with the facts.

According to Zephaniah 3:17, she has a Father who is mighty to save, who takes great delight in her: a Father who, when she meets with Him in His Word, promises to quiet her with His love and rejoice over her with singing.

Per God's Word, she has an empathetic High Priest in Jesus (Heb. 4:8) who comforts her as she weeps (2 Cor. 1:4) and catches her every tear in His bottle (Ps. 56:8). Revelation 21:4 states this same High Priest promises her that one day He will wipe her tears away for good, abolish death once and for all, and usher in a new age of life and laughter and rejoicing.

Ephesians 2:4–5 reminds her that she cannot travel so far that His mercy can't reach her.

Psalm 138:8 assures her that His plans for her will never be thwarted.

Though she has surely felt lonely at times, Psalm 139:5 insists that she has never, for one fraction of a second, been alone.

Neither have you.

He goes before you, walks beside you and upholds you with His mighty right hand. He strengthens you, helps you, and fights for you.

If you are in Christ, then supernatural power resides in you and that power is unleashed as we seek Him in His Word.

What was the last thing He said to you? When was the last time you sat at His feet to listen, learn, and lean into the One who loves you?

As I type, I have not heard again from Bridgette, but my prayer for her is the same prayer I pray for you, my children, my husband, and myself. It's not original or elaborate, but it was breathed by the Spirit and penned by His psalmist:

> Open [our] eyes that [we] may see wonderful things in your law.
>
> —Psalm 119:18 NIV

THE DINNER PARTY

I should have listened to my mother.

Manners were important to her as my sisters and I were growing up. We knew to say "please" and "thank you" and to look grown-ups in the eyes. She taught us to shake hands, answer questions in full sentences, and to ask polite questions to show that we were interested in the amused adult to whom we were speaking.

Never did a dinner gathering go by that we weren't given jobs—opening the door, stashing purses and coats, and taking gifts and dishes into the kitchen.

That last one was important and taught me a lesson that my mother, the gracious Beverly Ashbrook, later reiterated:

Never ever attend a party empty-handed!

It's the golden rule of hospitality, regardless of what the invitation says. So when we received a colorful evite, I should've known better.

"Dinner Party!" the e-mail read. "Six o'clock sharp at so-and-so's house."

We hadn't seen so-and-so in several months, so I eagerly checked the "yes" box and promptly asked what I could bring.

An hour later, my phone chirped, indicating a text message.

"So glad you can come," said so-and-so, "it's been way too long!"

"I know!" I wrote back, and added, "Can't wait!" with plenty of smiley-faced emoticons to indicate my excitement.

She answered back with a smiley face of her own, and that's when I remembered that she hadn't answered my question. I hastily typed,

"What can I bring?"

"Not a thing!" she replied.

"You sure?" I shot back.

"Just your happy selves, I've got it all covered," she wrote, with a flurry of smiley faces and hearts.

Laughing, I put my phone down.

Several weeks later, Mike and I kissed our kids goodbye, gave final instructions to the babysitter, and pulled out of the driveway.

"I hate that we're not bringing anything," I told my husband. "It doesn't feel right."

Mike leaves that kind of thing to me, so he glanced my way and asked, "Well, want to stop and grab something?"

"No, she said not to," I said. "Besides, we're already running late."

I should've listened to my gut. If not my gut, then my mother's voice ringing through my mind, insisting over and over that you "never, *ever* attend a party empty-handed."

Each guest brought something—a bottle of wine, a tray of desserts, or a little gift. And I was absolutely mortified.

Our friends were delighted to see us and as gracious as could be as we left, thanking us for carving out the time, getting a sitter, and making the drive.

"Let's not let so many months go by before next time," my husband said, clapping his buddy on the back.

One last hug, a promise to call soon, and we were in the car on our way back to Flower Mound.

I turned to my husband as we turned out of their neighborhood. "I am so embarrassed!"

"What? Why?" His look was one of genuine confusion.

"Why?" I half-yelled. "We were the only people who didn't bring anything, *that's* why!"

Mike furrowed his brow, trying to figure out my sudden burst of emotion. "But you told me they said not to," he said.

"I know, but I know better," I wailed. "It's the golden rule of hospitality! You never go to a party empty-handed!"

Mike shook his head. "Then why didn't you bring something?"

I'm not sure, but at one point I might have seen my husband shiver from the cold shoulder he got on the rest of the ride home.

What would you say if I told you that you and I tend to treat our relationship with God like a dinner party?

Here's the deal.

Salvation—our eternal life in heaven with God the Father, Jesus the Son, and the Holy Spirit—was a free gift. And if you earn a gift it's not a gift; it's a reward. Since our salvation is a gift and not a reward, that means we did nothing to get it.

Nothing.

Here's how I know:

> As for you, you were dead in your transgressions and sins, in which you used to live when you followed the ways of this world and of the ruler of the kingdom of the air, the spirit who is now at work in those who are disobedient. All of us also lived among them at one time, gratifying the cravings of our flesh and following its desires and thoughts. Like the rest, we were by nature deserving of wrath. But because of his great love for us, God, who is rich in mercy, made us alive with Christ even when we were dead in transgressions—it is by grace you have been saved.
>
> —Ephesians 2:1–5

Note especially the first verse. "As for you, you were dead . . ." it says. The last time I checked, dead people don't do much. They don't have sudden, spontaneous bursts of revelation, and they don't make faith decisions. They also don't get up and walk down church aisles on their own to receive the Lord.

Those are things that happen *after* God, "who is rich in mercy," bestows a saving faith upon us.

No.

You and I did nothing to earn our salvation, and we certainly didn't deserve it. The text says not only were we dead, but we were dead in our "transgressions and sins." Romans 5:8 echoes this sentiment, stating that God proved His love for us by sending Christ to die for us "while we were still sinners."

You and I have been invited to the eternal Promised Land, and the only thing we bring to the party, as it has been said, is the sin that makes our salvation necessary.

The implications of this are huge.

It means we can stop striving to please God and start resting and rejoicing in the finished work of Christ. We can cease this endless struggle to earn and keep what is ours by grace.

God is already pleased with us because He is fully pleased with Christ, and we can't do anything to add to it.

Thousands of years ago, God spoke to the prophet Ezekiel about this very thing:

> For I will take you out of the nations; I will gather you from all the countries and bring you back into your own land. I will sprinkle clean water on you, and you will be clean; I will cleanse you from all your impurities and from all your idols. I will give you a new heart and put a new spirit in you; I will remove from you your heart of stone and give you a heart of flesh. And I will put my Spirit in you and move you to follow my decrees and be careful to keep my laws. Then you will live in the land I gave your ancestors; you will be my people, and I will be your God. I will save you from all your uncleanness. I will call for the grain and make it plentiful and will not bring famine upon you. I will increase the fruit of the trees and the crops of the field, so that you will no longer suffer disgrace among the nations because of famine.
>
> —Ezekiel 36:24 –30 NIV

Notice how many times God says "I will." I counted twelve times in seven verses. Just to recap, God says that He, not us, will

- Remove us from where we don't belong.

- Place us where we do belong.

- Cleanse us from sin and idolatry.

- Give a new heart and a new spirit.

- Remove our cold heart of sin.

- Place His Spirit in us.
- Move our hearts to obey.
- Be our personal Savior.
- Save us from our ongoing propensity to sin.
- Provide for our needs.

Jesus calls us to obey, and we must. But a life of obedience happens one of two ways, and only one is sustainable: fueled by fear, endlessly striving to earn God's favor, or fueled by grace because we already have it.

Let this revive our hearts and renew our spirit. This is one party where we truly can't bring a thing.

THE GLOW STICK

Neither do people light a lamp and put it under a bowl. Instead they put it on its stand, and it gives light to everyone in the house.

—Matthew 5:15

If you've ever spent any time on the Texas coast, you've heard of ghost crabbin'. We were first introduced to the "sport" in summer 2015 when we ran into a friend of Mike's in Port Aransas.

We happened to be staying in the same condos—our first night was their last, and Mike was delighted to bump into him.

"Billy! What are you doing here, man?"

Billy laughed, giving each of us a Texas-sized bear hug in turn. "I've got the whole family down here, buddy! We're havin' one last hoo-rah down at the beach tonight. Ya gotta come! There's about twenty little ones—plenty of playmates for these hooligans."

Nick looked uncertain as Billy tussled his hair.

"Seriously," Billy said, stooping to my son's level. "Ever been ghost crabbin'?"

Both of my children shook their heads.

"Then it's settled. Y'all come on down around nine o'clock. We're making hot dogs, s'mores, and as soon as that sun goes down, we're grabbing flashlights and huntin' ghost crabs."

Caitlyn's face lit up, and she looked at me as if to ask, "Can we, Mama, can we?" I nodded and smiled.

"You gotta be quick, though," he continued, sizing the kids up. "You quick?"

"I'm the fastest runner on my whole baseball team," boasted Nick.

"Then I expect you to get a whole lotta crabs, buddy!" Billy patted Nick on the back, and this time he didn't squirm away.

"Nine o'clock, then?"

At nine o'clock on the dot we crossed the bridge over the dunes and scanned the beach for Billy's group.

"There they are," my husband pointed out, and the kids ran off, brand new shiny plastic buckets in one hand, flashlights clutched in the other.

The group greeted us warmly, offering us drinks and hot dogs. A meticulous sand castle project was underway on one side of us, a lively game of beach volleyball on the other. I sat quietly next to Mike, listening as he and Billy laughed and caught up.

By ten o'clock the group deemed it dark enough for ghost crabbing, so Billy's oldest son rallied the troops, pointing different directions and giving instructions.

"We do this every year."

I jumped, startled out of my reverie by a friendly voice.

Billy's wife smiled and introduced herself.

Standing up, I returned the introduction and thanked her for her hospitality.

"We're so glad to bump into you," she replied graciously. "Billy has mentioned Mike many times." She turned her gaze toward the children, then said, "I know they have flashlights, but it was making me nervous to have the kids running around in the dark, so this year I insisted they wear glow sticks."

As if on cue, the kids started tearing open packages and cracking their sticks. They made them into headbands, bracelets, and necklaces. One boy, about thirteen, broke two and shoved a stick up each nostril.

"Look, Mom, I'm a walrus," he yelled, laughing hysterically as his mother shook her head.

Five more minutes and the kids were off. Except for a few campfires, the beach was almost completely dark. The children had grouped themselves into glowing clusters of four or five and were racing down the beach, screaming and giggling.

After chatting for a few more minutes, someone hollered for Billy's wife, and she politely excused herself. Sitting back down, I alternated between stargazing and kid watching.

The glow sticks were truly genius. We knew precisely how many kids there were—twenty-four—and I could count exactly twenty-four sets of moving neon bands.

Call me crazy, but I think the glow stick holds some theological implications for you and me.

> You are the light of the world. A town built on a hill cannot be hidden.
>
> —Matthew 5:14

The way the glow stick works is like this: The plastic tube contains two chemicals and a dye. Inside the plastic tube is a smaller glass tube filled with hydrogen peroxide. Surrounding the glass is our second chemical, diphenyl oxalate, mixed with the dye. When the two substances combine, voilà! You have the glowing neon band we wave at parties and concerts.

Something has to happen, though, before the glow stick can operate at its full potential.

You have to break it.

The great A. W. Tozer once said, "It is doubtful whether God can bless a man greatly until He has hurt him deeply."[15]

I think of some of the women I work shoulder to shoulder with in ministry. There's the girl from DC who grew up without a mother or a sense of self-worth. She gave herself over to drugs and men, but everything changed when she met Jesus.

She is about to become a certified biblical counselor with a ferocious desire to minister to young women.

There's the woman who suffered abuse as a young teen and had an abortion in her early twenties. After her husband had left her with

---

15 "A. W. Tozer," Goodreads, accessed August 17, 2016, https://www.goodreads.com/author/quotes/1082290.A_W_Tozer.

four young children, she wanted to die. Instead, she turned to Christ. She has now authored over ten books, speaks at conferences nationwide, and hosted a DVD series to encourage women that they can live again after the pain of divorce.

There's the man who grew up with a poor excuse for a father. Instead of wallowing in the pain and walking in his dad's footsteps, he surrendered His life to the Lord. He operates a large Christian mentoring program for elementary- and middle school-aged boys and has been granted permission into the public school system.

I think of my own past, a past I'd like to forget. Years and years of self-medicating my undiagnosed generalized anxiety, trying everything and anything to escape the confines of my mind. Years of poor choices and tangles to work through.

Yet God has not let one ounce of my pain go to waste. He replaced it with compassion, empathy, and an insatiable hunger for His Word.

Every one of us—every last one of us—is broken. The question is *what will we do with our brokenness?*

Our sin left unconfessed will haunt us. It will keep us up at night, invade our peace, and inhibit us from realizing our Kingdom potential. But when we come humbly before our Heavenly Father, acknowledging our inability to do it right, get it right, and say the right thing, He turns our pain into purpose and our trials into testimonies.

Every last one of us is broken. Sin has infested our very DNA. That is why Jesus had to hang, broken, on the cross, so that sin might be put to death and we might walk in the light of redemption.

Perhaps you find yourself battered, bruised, and heavy with shame. Be encouraged, my friend. There is no hurt He can't heal, no wound He can't mend, and no sin that outweighs His grace. You are never so broken that you can't shine for the glory of God.

> When Jesus spoke again to the people, he said, 'I am the light of the world. Whoever follows me will never walk in darkness, but will have the light of life.'
>
> —John 8:12

THE BACKPACK

And my God will supply all your needs according to His riches in glory in Christ Jesus.

—Philippians 4:19 NASB

I have been accused of hoarding.

It's true. Anytime my sisters drive down from Kansas City to visit, we inevitably end up combing through my closet. Not because I want to, but because they think it's funny.

Here's the deal. I do not hoard. I just don't like to throw anything away if there is a chance I might use it again.

Sigh.

Okay, maybe it's *mild* hoarding.

I can remember one time in particular. My youngest sister, Emily, was rooting through my jeans.

"Rebecca!" she exclaimed in horror, "Didn't you buy these in *high school*?"

She held up the most comfortable pair of blue jeans I have ever had the pleasure of wearing.

"Yes, but they're in good shape," I protested, "There's no reason to throw them away!"

"They're from 1991," yelled my sister. "That is your reason!"

That day we pulled old running shoes, purses, belts, and anything that hadn't been worn in a year out of my closet and sent it off to Goodwill.

My husband would tell you that my "collections" aren't limited to clothing. Stuffed in a closet are nearly every art project my children have ever created, along with half-read books, half-finished knitting projects, and other things I'm sure I'll get to someday.

Which brings me to my laptop bag.

I had carried a laptop bag for nearly ten years when I decided, *on my own*, thank you very much, that it was time to get a new one. The thing had holes in the corners and unraveling seams, so I asked for a new one for Christmas.

Correction—I asked for a nice, sophisticated black briefcase-like laptop bag that I could take to both work and speaking engagements. Something that would make me look professional.

Sure enough, on Christmas morning, there was a large beautifully wrapped package with my name on it.

After the kids had torn through their gifts, I smiled at my husband and sang, "I bet I know what this is!"

Mike, who puts more thought, time, and effort into gift-giving than anyone I know, grinned and leaned forward in eager expectation.

I ripped off the paper, tossed it aside, and pulled out a backpack.

A large, red and black, Swiss Army-brand backpack.

My husband immediately set about showing me all the bells and whistles, pockets and compartments that the backpack boasted. To be sure, there was a nook and cranny for everything, from my cell phone to my car keys to, well, anything else I wanted to throw in it.

Now don't get me wrong. It was a great backpack. It's just that I hadn't wanted a backpack.

I had wanted a nice, sophisticated black briefcase-like laptop bag that I could take to both work and speaking engagements. You know, something that made me look like a grown-up, not a college kid.

Although I did my best to seem excited, Mike knew better.

"You can always exchange it for a laptop bag," he said, "but do me a favor and just try it. I think something like this is going to end up being more practical."

As it turns out, he was right.

You might read this and think, "What kind of husband would pick that kind of gift?"

The kind of husband who knows his wife and knows what she needs.

Mike knows that I suffer from chronic back and neck pain, sometimes so severe that I can barely turn my head. He sees me shift my purse from one shoulder to another in discomfort, as carrying anything on one side of my body for too long hurts. A laptop would weigh me down, whereas a backpack would evenly distribute the weight.

While I was thinking about speaking engagements, Mike was thinking about the long trek from car to class at Dallas Theological Seminary, where I study. He knew that I needed something that would carry textbooks, Bibles, and notepads, in addition to my computer.

I was focused on a want, but my husband answered my need.

How glad I am that he did.

How grateful I am that God is the same way.

Over and over again throughout the pages of Scripture, we see that the God of the Bible is the God who meets the deepest needs of His people.

Take the Samaritan woman at the well in John, chapter 4.

With only her physical thirst in mind, she lugs her bucket to the watering hole during the heat of the day. There she finds a tired and thirsty Jesus who asks for a drink.

The drink leads to a conversation that leads to a confession—this woman, who has been married five times, is currently living with a man who is not her husband.

She needed more than water for washing and drinking.

She needed Living Water for mercy, forgiveness, and redemption.

She came wanting water, and Jesus, loving her more than any other person on the planet ever had or ever would, sent her away with salvation.

What have you longed for and not received? There is rest knowing that the author of your salvation is also the author of your story. He sees around the corners of your life you are not privy to. He knows all the bumps and bends in the road ahead and that, sometimes, the best way is through the darkest valleys.

He knows that comfort breeds complacency while trials produce a testimony. He leads us to quiet waters for refreshing, and then back through the wilderness for testing.

What might our lives look like if we had the faith to believe that

He loves us enough to forsake some of our deepest wants for our most dire needs?

I wear my big black and red Swiss Army backpack with pride, regardless of where I am going. Not only is it a great gift from my husband, but also a reminder that I love and trust a God who has promised to meet our every need.

And sometimes our wants, too.

> Jesus stopped and ordered the man to be brought to him. When he came near, Jesus asked him, "What do you want me to do for you?"
>
> "Lord, I want to see," he replied.
>
> Jesus said to him, "Receive your sight; your faith has healed you." Immediately he received his sight and followed Jesus, praising God. When all the people saw it, they also praised God.
>
> —Luke 18:40–43 NIV

THE ROCKY MOUNTAINS

For you will go out with joy and be led forth with peace;
The mountains and the hills will break forth into shouts of
joy before you, And all the trees of the field will clap their
hands.

—Isaiah 55:12 NASB

As a broadcaster and speaker who makes a living running her
mouth, it's unusual to find me at a loss for words. There is, however, a
question with which I struggle.

"Where are you from?"

This is where I typically smile, sigh, and say, "So many states to
choose from. Where to begin?"

I won't bore you with the list, but my family of origin relocated, on
average, every three years.

There are benefits and detriments to moving around so much. On
the social front, I am comfortable in new situations. I am not easily
intimidated, and while I am an introvert, I'm not shy.

On the flip side, uprooting so many times has made maintaining
friendships across time and distance difficult. You would think the
opposite to be true, perhaps, but relationships can be hard for me to
maintain. I let go too easily and have regretted not investing in people
on a deeper level. If I were to play amateur psychologist, I would guess
that this stems from self-protective motivations. Saying goodbye so
many times over the years has caused a wall to spring up around my
heart, one the Lord (and therapists) have been systematically chipping
away at over the last few years.

It was the desire to reinvest in my high school friendships that led me back to Highlands Ranch, Colorado, in summer 2015. There is a special sweetness found with those who knew you in your younger years, before time and titles set in and identities form from outside forces.

There were about ten of us in our tight-knit group, and most of them had stayed in Colorado after high school and college. Since graduating in 1992, we had all gotten married, had kids, and started careers. In the busyness of life and with several states between us, I had slowly let the friendships fade.

I'm not sure what changed. Perhaps it was when Kelley, my best friend and one of our little tribe members, passed away. Maybe it was because I wanted to show the crew that, while I had been a mess in high school, I had managed, by God's grace, to turn things around. Part of it was simply wanting my husband to know more about that chunk of my life. Relatively speaking, it was a short season—we lived in Highlands Ranch for only four years, but those years profoundly affected and shaped the person I was to become.

As the trip approached, my excitement grew. I had meticulously planned out every moment. Thursday night Mike and I would spend a night out in Denver to celebrate our eleventh anniversary. The next morning we would walk around the city, shopping and sightseeing. Then we would meet my Aunt Cia at her high-rise condo in the heart of the city, where we would stay for the remainder of the trip.

Friday night was dinner with Vicki and Trent; Saturday, lunch with Brandon; and then Saturday evening we would head to the home of one of my dearest friends, Becky, where we would meet her family and have dinner.

There was one thing that I didn't expect—one thing that caught me off guard and sent shock waves through my mind.

The sight of the Rocky Mountains—towering and majestic with snow-topped peaks even in the middle of July. As the plane descended, my husband and I craned our necks to catch a better glimpse. Mike expressed his awe, and I wondered this to myself:

How in the world have I forgotten how

breathtaking these mountains are?

I thought back to 1989 when our family of five loaded up a moving truck and our mini-van and made the drive from Minnesota. Having not seen the mountains since I was a very little girl, and scarcely remembering the trip, they sucked the breath right out of my fifteen-year-old lungs.

The house we moved into sat high on a hill with a perfect, uninterrupted view of the Rockies. I remember eating breakfast on our second-story deck and thinking how grateful I was that we had moved to Colorado.

I wonder when I stopped regarding them as spectacular. At what point did the mountains become ordinary? How long did it take for my eyes to adjust to their majesty and for their splendidness to fade to mundane?

The thought nagged at me through the course of the trip.

We had a wonderful time with my old cronies. Mike fit right in, and it was as though no time had passed at all, as is often the case with true friends. We promised to keep in touch and not wait so long for the next visit.

As Mike and I boarded the plane, I asked him if I could have the window seat. I wanted to look at the mountains as long as possible, not knowing when we would be back.

The plane ascended, and the mountains slipped from sight, so I took out my journal and opened my Bible. I quickly flipped through the pages until I found the passage I was looking for—Ezekiel's vision of the throne room of the Almighty God:

> Then there came a voice from above the vault over their heads as they stood with lowered wings. Above the vault over their heads was what looked like a throne of lapis lazuli, and high above on the throne was a figure like that of a man. I saw that from what appeared to be his waist up he looked like glowing metal, as if full of fire, and that from there down he looked like fire; and brilliant light surrounded him. Like the appearance of a rainbow in the clouds on a rainy day, so was the radiance around him. This was the

appearance of the likeness of the glory of the Lord. When I saw it, I fell facedown, and I heard the voice of one speaking.

—Ezekiel 1:25–28 NIV

Although I'd read these words many times, highlighting and underlining them in my Bible, I saw them as if for the first time. One phrase, in particular, caught my attention: "This was the appearance of the *likeness* of the glory of the Lord." This wasn't even His glory—simply the likeness of it, and the prophet fell *facedown*.

As I continued to read, a thought sliced through my mind with the sharp blade of conviction. Just as the Rocky Mountains had become ordinary when we lived near Denver, so had the Lord and the miracle of my salvation become something I'd taken for granted. No longer worthy of beholding as magnificent, but something I'd walked with for so long that it had ceased to strike wonder in my heart.

The next two verses in Ezekiel drove the point home:

He said to me, "Son of man, stand up on your feet and I will speak to you." As he spoke, the Spirit came into me and raised me to my feet, and I heard him speaking to me.

—Ezekiel 2:1–2

Although I haven't researched the topic exhaustively, I think it's safe to say that nearly every time in Scripture one is faced with the Lord in His glory, they fall facedown faster than you can blink. Of note in this passage is that Ezekiel would've stayed in that position indefinitely had the Spirit not intervened.

I don't think the prophet ever got over that vision. The Lord called him to prophesy in strange and unusual ways, bringing an unwelcome message to an ungrateful people. Ezekiel always obeyed. While the text does not tell us, I imagine that he held the vision of the Lord in His splendor always before him. Knowing how he would spend eternity, what could a mere man do to him that would cause him to turn from God?

How I wish I could say the same for myself. While I know that Jesus saved me while I was yet a sinner, I find myself trying to earn His favor. I know that heaven awaits, but I still cling to the things of this world. I know that, because I am hidden securely in Christ, my Heavenly Father fully approves of me, but I still strive ceaselessly for the approval of man.

I have failed to keep the vision of God in His splendor before me. I have not stopped down nearly often enough to gaze upon His majesty. The scars upon my Savior's hands have ceased to drive me to my knees, and it's been too long since I, with sweet, doubting Thomas, traced the wound on His side that paid for my sins.

Do you find yourself in a dry place? Has complacency replaced joy, and faith become routine?

Let us behold the beauty of Christ with new eyes. Let us plead with the Lord to revive our hearts and renew our devotion. He is the God who makes all things new—including our desire to know Him! May the fullness of Him drive out the "us-ness" of us, and let our lives flow out of gratitude and grace.

> I turned around to see the voice that was speaking to me. And when I turned I saw seven golden lampstands, 13 and among the lampstands was someone like a son of man, dressed in a robe reaching down to his feet and with a golden sash around his chest. The hair on his head was white like wool, as white as snow, and his eyes were like blazing fire. His feet were like bronze glowing in a furnace, and his voice was like the sound of rushing waters. In his right hand he held seven stars, and coming out of his mouth was a sharp, double-edged sword. His face was like the sun shining in all its brilliance. When I saw him, I fell at his feet as though dead. Then he placed his right hand on me and said: "Do not be afraid. I am the First and the Last. I am the Living One; I was dead, and now look, I am alive for ever and ever! And I hold the keys of death and Hades.

> —Revelation 1:12–18

THE BROKEN ANTENNAE

For what great nation is there that has a god so near to it as is the LORD our God whenever we call on Him?

—Deuteronomy 4:7 NASB

In an article posted on *ChristianityToday.com,* columnist Andy Crouch observes that "an American thirteen-year-old today has never known a day without the Internet, mobile technology, and social media. He or she started kindergarten the year the iPhone™ was released and Facebook opened its site to the public."[16]

Neither my daughter nor my son learned the art of stretching the phone cord as far as it can possibly go to get as far as you can possibly get from adult ears while actually talking—a lost art in itself—on the phone.

They have always been able to chat with out-of-state relatives face-to-face via computer rather than wait until after seven o'clock at night for the long distance rates to go down.

They have only known Google Maps, never had to search for the Mapsco coordinates, or, better yet, never tried to fold the road atlas back up the way it initially was.

Their memories of combing the aisles at the video store are foggy at best, and they have never known anything other than the crystal-clear,

16 Andy Crouch, "The Return of Shame," *Christianity Today,* March, 10, 2015, http://www.christianitytoday.com/ct/2015/march/andy-crouch-gospel-in-age-of-public-shame.html?utm_source=ctdirect-html&utm_medium=Newsletter&utm_term=11609528&utm_content=340686743&utm_campaign=2013.

high-def picture of the skinny flat-screen TV.

If you are of my generation you remember the rabbit ears.

The first TV I can recall was black and white with two knobs—one for channels 2–13 (VHF) and the other for channels 14–83 (UHF). If memory serves, the UHF channels were about as useless as a white crayon on butcher paper, offering only squiggly lines and static.

I remember moving the antennae every which way to get the clearest picture possible of *The Brady Bunch,* one of two after school programs offered between 3:00 and 4:00 p.m. I also remember when the antennae broke.

Try as we might to make a coat hanger work, once the antennae was broken, the TV was useless. We could get sporadic bursts of sound, but no picture reception whatsoever.

It was after the loss of a cherished friend I realized that, just like my family's old television set, you and I have broken antennas.

I sat across from Terry Dorsey and Mark "Hawkeye" Louis every weekday morning from the hours of five-thirty to ten for nearly a decade. Dorsey's golden voice woke millions of North Texans up for over thirty-five years. He was the first person I told when I "finally went on a good date" that ultimately resulted in my marriage. When I walked down the aisle to say "I do" to Mike Carrell, he was there.

He was there through two difficult pregnancies, two precious "birth-days," and one nasty case of post-partum depression. Every day for almost ten years, he was there for the highs, the lows, and everything in between.

He listened when I explained my call into ministry and blessed me as I left. And whether or not management would consent to it, he left the door wide open should I ever want to return to the Dorsey Gang.

Losing him was like losing a family member. It felt like a punch to the soul.

The morning after I found out, I had to be back on the radio on 90.9 KCBI, and I was not feeling it.

The week following the news was a whirlwind of media and funeral preparations, topped off by a weekend of remembrance.

I never felt God's presence. Not at the visitation, not at the funeral, and not at the grave site.

Not even once.

I asked the Lord to comfort Terry's family, and I believe He did and *is*. The service was beautiful—the perfect mix of laughter and tears. I hugged and embraced his wife and grandkids, encouraging them as best I could.

But inside I felt hollow.

The next day I had to stand up in front of a large audience and teach out of Ephesians.

I felt like a hypocrite.

It wasn't that I didn't believe.

I believed.

I knew He was there. I knew He was near. I knew He was close to the brokenhearted and that He saved those who were crushed in spirit.[17]

But I didn't *feel* it.

The next day was a Monday and I could sense the Lord wanted me to spend quiet time with Him. Instead, I called my friend Lisa and met her for lunch.

Tuesday morning I began my forty-five minute commute into downtown Dallas and tried to pray. It felt like I was shouting to an empty room, so I gave up and recited Scripture instead. I had been memorizing Ephesians, chapter 5, but almost without thought, started speaking Romans 8 instead.

By the time I hit verse 38, tears were rolling down my cheeks.

> For I am convinced that neither death nor life, neither angels nor demons, neither the present nor the future, nor any powers, neither height nor depth, nor anything else in all creation, will be able to separate us from the love of God that is in Christ Jesus our Lord.
>
> —Romans 8:38–39 NIV

As I voiced the words God breathed, He spoke to me. He reminded

---

17 Psalm 34:18 NIV

me that my antenna is broken, and just because my receptors were off didn't mean that He wasn't speaking to me, whispering words of comfort and consolation.

Do you ever feel like God's not there? Like your prayers echo around the empty chambers of the heavenlies and your tears fall unnoticed? Then you need this as much as I do.

The presence of pain in no way, shape, or form suggests the absence of God. Our ability to feel Him is never indicative of His nearness.

This is why we walk by faith, not by feelings.

Emotions are a beautiful, wonderful, awful gift. They carry us to the heights only to drop us in the depths. Emotions are unreliable, unreasonable, and ever-changing. God is ever-present, everlasting, and never-changing.

Our awareness of Him has no bearing on His activity in our lives. The danger of seeking after God experiences is that the experiences often come at the expense of concentrated time seeking God in His Word.

Experiences will not carry us through the depths, but His Word will.

It was through speaking His Word I remembered that even though I felt a chasm between myself and the Most High, no such chasm existed, for nothing can separate me from His love: Not death, not life. Not angels, not demons. My past cannot separate me from Him, and neither can my present circumstances or my future sins. Height cannot come between us, and neither can depth.

Neither can my grief.

Or my depression.

Or my pitiful attempt to process it all.

The next time you stand on the precipice of the emotional chasm, dive. Dive deeply into God's Word and saturate yourself with His Presence. Don't know where to start? How about here:

> Praise be to the God and Father of our Lord Jesus Christ, the Father of compassion and the God of all comfort, who comforts us in all our troubles, so that we can comfort those in any trouble with the comfort we ourselves receive from God. For just as we share abundantly in the sufferings of

Christ, so also our comfort abounds through Christ. If we are distressed, it is for your comfort and salvation; if we are comforted, it is for your comfort, which produces in you patient endurance of the same sufferings we suffer. And our hope for you is firm, because we know that just as you share in our sufferings, so also you share in our comfort.

—2 Corinthians 1:3–7

The ever-present, everlasting, and never-changing God that we call Father may not deliver you from your circumstances, but He will never leave you alone in them, regardless of whether or not your spiritual antennae is working. And His Word promises that He will repurpose and repackage your pain, putting it to future-use, for your good and His glory.

Praise be to God.

The Lord is near to the brokenhearted and saves those who are crushed in spirit.

—Psalm 34:18 NASB

BLUE BUNNY

Teacher, which is the greatest commandment in the Law? Jesus replied: "'Love the Lord your God with all your heart and with all your soul and with all your mind.' This is the first and greatest commandment. And the second is like it: 'Love your neighbor as yourself.' All the Law and the Prophets hang on these two commandments."

—Matthew 22:36–40 NIV

Do you remember your favorite childhood comfy toy?

I don't remember it well, but my parents tell me I had a blanket that I called my "mackey." Mackey was my constant nighttime companion. No mackey, no sleepy.

One of my sisters had a doll named Baby Beth. In the hectic chaos of packing for three little girls and herself, my mother didn't notice when Baby Beth got left behind on a three-week trip to Florida.

My sister noticed. When bedtime came with no Baby Beth to be found, my father heard my little sister's tantrum all the way up in Minnesota.

I suppose it helped that he was on the phone with my mom at the time.

Ever the hero, my dad packed up the worn and tattered doll and overnighted it to Florida the next day.

My two children also had their comfy toys. A girlfriend of mine gave Caitlyn a beautiful, plush pink blanket when she was born. At eighteen months, my daughter named it "pink blankey." Another friend gave my son a soft baby-blue bunny. I can still see it—my sweet, chubby two-year-old boy toddling around, plump fingers wrapped around the velveteen ears, dragging that bunny around the house.

I wonder how many hours my husband and I logged frantically searching for blue bunny and pink blankey: how many panicked calls to my mother or sisters, trying to figure out where their comfy toys got lost.

Blue bunny and pink blankey are still around, though they've lost their status in my kids' eyes. The baby blanket has seen better days. The rabbit's fur, once softer than silk, is now matted and worn, thanks to countless trips through the laundry. The delicate blue is now closer to a grimy gray. No longer nighttime companions, the comfy toys have been relegated from the bedroom to a toy chest somewhere.

Some time ago I was on a laser-focused mission to declutter the house. It was an all-out assault on excess—if we didn't need it, didn't use it, whatever "it" was had to go.

I attacked each room with feverish intensity, stuffing things into boxes and garbage bags. No room for mercy. No time for sentimentality. A storewide going-out-of-business sale where all items must go.

And then, there it was. Stuffed back in a far corner on the floor, beneath the bottom shelf of our hall closet, a glimpse of grimy gray-blue. My fingers closed on what once had been soft, velvet-like fur, and I pulled out blue bunny.

At that moment my resolve melted away. I sat there on the floor staring at what had once been irreplaceable to Nick. My eyes filled with tears as memories flashed before my eyes. Me, cradling my son, rocking him to sleep as he clutched his stuffed toy in his arms. Nick, crying out in the middle of the night that he couldn't find blue bunny. Mike, running back in the house before we left to visit my sisters in Kansas City because a little boy forgot his rabbit.

That bunny wasn't grimy; it was *loved*. It had been lavished with the pure, unfiltered love of a little boy; the kind of love that won't let go.

The kind of love that leaves a mark.

> See what great love the Father has lavished on us, that we should be called children of God! And that is what we are!

The reason the world does not know us is that it did not know him.

—1 John 3:1

It was bizarre, what happened to me there on the floor. All of a sudden my heart swelled with love for that worn-out stuffed animal, and there was no way I was letting it go.

Not because it had any inherent value. Not because it was aesthetically pleasing to the eye.

Simply because my son loved it, and I love my son with all my heart.

When you love someone wholeheartedly, you also love what they love.

Could it be that we don't love each other well because we don't love our Heavenly Father as we should?

Jesus instructs us to love God with our whole heart, soul, and mind. John, the Beloved Apostle, wrote that God has lavished us with love. Not simply an emotive, warm and fuzzy love, but a determined love: a purpose-filled love. It's a love that sets its face like flint, a love that won't swerve from its course. It's a love that wrings itself out, a love that spends itself, a love that sacrifices.

Love without boundaries or borders; love that lasts, that never fails, that won't let go.

The kind of love that leaves a mark.

Not matted fur or tattered ears, but whip-lashed skin and a pierced side.

Thorn marks. Scorn marks. Nail marks.

If we are loved with a love like that, how much more so should we love others?

Our culture doesn't need more lectures or laws—it needs more love. But the kind of love we need can't be mustered up by bearing down and trying harder. That's not love—that's behavior modification that only works until the next person offends us, or cuts us off in traffic, or makes us feel marginalized.

I've heard it said that we become what we behold.

If that's true, and I believe it is, then the answer isn't trying harder.

It's beholding the scars of our Savior.

It's gazing upon the face of Christ and finding Him lovelier than our right to be right. It's spending time in the Word of God and allowing it to change us, one degree at a time, into His image.

It's allowing His love for us to turn us upside-down and inside-out. It's asking Him to help us love Him more and to love His own through us. It's giving Him all access to our hearts and minds so that we can be His hands and feet.

Blue bunny and pink blankey were irreplaceable to my children, priceless items worth more than silver or gold. They loved their comfy toys, and so do I.

I wouldn't sell them for anything, wouldn't part with them no matter what.

It makes no sense, other than I love my children, and because I do, what is precious to them is precious to me.

You are irreplaceable to Jesus. He bought you at a high price and holds you in His warm embrace. We cannot repay Him, and until He returns, there is only one way to love Him back.

By loving those He loves. By cherishing His image-bearers, serving His children, and seeking out those who don't know Him yet.

Is it difficult?

Let's not kid ourselves. We are broken people living in a broken world, and we tend to break almost everything we touch—including each other. But Christ has committed to finishing what He started on the cross, and that is reconciling His people to His Father through the hearts of you and me.

> This is how we know what love is: Jesus Christ laid down his life for us. And we ought to lay down our lives for our brothers and sisters. If anyone has material possessions and sees a brother or sister in need but has no pity on them, how can the love of God be in that person? Dear children, let us not love with words or speech but with actions and in truth.
>
> —1 John 3:16–18

NO NEW BEGINNINGS
(AND WHY THAT'S GOOD NEWS)

From that time Jesus began to show His disciples that He must go to Jerusalem, and suffer many things from the elders and chief priests and scribes, and be killed, and be raised up on the third day.

—Matthew 16:21 NASB

We sat there silently at the kitchen table in our home on Churchill Street in Shoreview, Minnesota. It shouldn't have surprised me. We'd done this before, many times, in fact.

I should have seen it coming, but I didn't.

My father's words hit me like a cold bucket of ice water in the face. We were moving. Again.

My middle sister immediately started crying, but I simply sat in silence.

"Girls, you will *love* Denver," my mother promised. "We're all going to learn how to ski."

As my mom started listing the attributes of Colorado, I began sifting through my mix of emotions: fear, shock, sorrow, bewilderment. New places and new faces. New lingo to learn and new hallways to navigate. But to my surprise, the feeling that rose to the top was a small sense of relief.

I had never fit in in Minnesota; high school, in particular, had been brutal. Colorado brought the unknown, but with the unknown came the promise of a new beginning.

I could turn a page and start afresh. No baggage, no history, just a clean slate, and a new chapter.

Highlands Ranch, Colorado, was a breath of fresh air. From our backyard deck, we had an uninterrupted view of the majestic Rocky Mountains. The high school I went to was small with new families moving in regularly, and in a relatively short time, I had a new circle of friends.

In one sense it was a new beginning, but in another, it wasn't at all. You see, I was still me.

Although I hadn't meant to, I had lugged the same insecurities across three state lines. The same demons that haunted me in Minnesota found me in Colorado. I didn't need a new beginning.

I needed someone to change the direction of my course. I needed a new ending.

Some have said that God is a god of new beginnings.

I would like to suggest otherwise.

The concept of a "new beginning" carries weighty expectations. In the car on the way to Colorado I remember thinking thoughts like this:

This time will be different.

This time I'll be better.

This time I'll try harder . . .

This time . . . this time . . . this time . . .

God cannot be the god of new beginnings because that would bring a new set of expectations: just another chance at the old demands, fully expecting that *this time* you'll get it right.

God does not come to you with new expectations. He always has and always will demand perfection. It's not enough to be good, getting better, or great, because the standard before us is holiness, and holiness cannot coexist with sin.

You and I can never meet the standard of holiness because, without outside intervention, we are an unholy people.

You and I have a sin-generator inside of us that never stops working. It runs twenty-four hours a day, seven days a week, fifty-two weeks a year. Don't believe me? Imagine for a moment that you had a news ticker running above you, broadcasting your every thought for all to see.

Imagine if the people closest to you knew what you really thought of them. Imagine what people would think if they knew the real motivation behind your good deeds.

I won't speak for *you*, but I would not be accepted in the circles I run in today, and I certainly wouldn't be allowed to do vocational ministry.

The Good News of the Gospel is this: Jesus did not go to the cross so you and I would be better. He didn't suffer crucifixion so you could have a "do-over."

God sent His Son to the cross because you and I need a new ending. Because we have a new ending, we have a new destination, and because we have a new destination, we have a new course set before us. Our new path carries no expectations because the expectations have been met perfectly in the person of Christ.

The standard of perfection was not lifted when Christ rose again. The demand remains the same. But if you are in Jesus, a beautiful transaction took place the moment you received Him as Savior: Your sin for His righteousness.

Our sin-generator doesn't turn off when we accept Christ. Our potential to fail on an epic level is ever-present, and we do well to remember it. But your punishment for your failures—past, present, and future—has forever been taken from you and for you.

We did the crime. Jesus did the time.

You do not need a new beginning, sweet friend, nor do you need a second chance. There are no do-overs with God; there is only done, finished, paid in full. For this reason, you are free to worship, free to serve, free to obey joyfully, and even free to fall and fail. When (and not if) you do, turn to Him, receive your grace, and rejoin the race, knowing that Christ finished in first place on your behalf.

So should we "sin all the more so that grace can abound?"[18] Are we free to quit the course? By no means. Being freed from the power of sin energizes us to run all the faster toward our new destination.

When you trip and fall, you don't return to the starting block to

---

18 Romans 6:15

start over, because God is not the god of new beginnings.

He is the God of new endings.

Our story is still being written.

We will go through trials, and we will have troubles. We will know sorrow and feel pain. We will drink from the bountiful cup of blessing and the bitter cup of loss.

Yes, your story is being written, but your ending is secured. You will indeed live happily-ever-after; joyfully, peacefully, and eternally in the Presence of Christ.

> After this, Jesus, knowing that all things had already been accomplished, to fulfill the Scripture, said, "I am thirsty." A jar full of sour wine was standing there; so they put a sponge full of the sour wine upon a branch of hyssop and brought it up to His mouth. Therefore when Jesus had received the sour wine, He said, "It is finished!" And He bowed His head and gave up His spirit.
>
> —John 19:28–30

DUMPSTER DIVING

Come, all you who are thirsty, come to the waters; and you who have no money, come, buy and eat! Come, buy wine and milk without money and without cost. Why spend money on what is not bread, and your labor on what does not satisfy? Listen, listen to me, and eat what is good, and you will delight in the richest of fare.

—Isaiah 55:1–2 NIV

"You just wouldn't believe how hard it is to get them to stop eating trash!"

If she didn't have my full attention before, she had it now.

It was the third day of the "God Crazy Freedom" conference, and I was spent. I was on the home stretch of a six-week run at a non-stop schedule that included a book launch, speaking several nights a week, and traveling three of the four weekends in October 2014. It was 1:15 p.m. on Saturday and I was running on caffeine and chocolate.

I had met Pastor Cindy Lange earlier that day. Pastor Cindy is on staff at The Secret Place in Springtown, Texas—a Christian facility that houses those in crisis. Their mission is simple:

To take in broken, shattered lives; to come alongside them; to help them get their feet under them, and to get them saved, cleaned up, and delivered; to put their lives back on track so they can walk in their deliverance.[19]

---

19 "About Us," *The Secret Place Ministry,* http://thesecretplaceministry.org/About%20Us.html.

The local police departments work with Cindy and will often call her when they find those they think she can help.

More often than not, they are homeless.

That's what Cindy and I were talking about.

Back to our conversation.

"You just wouldn't believe how hard it is to get them to stop eating trash!"

My eyes widened, and my jaw dropped.

"Really?" I asked incredulously, "Even when you are serving them meals?"

"Oh, yes," she replied. "It happens all the time. They'll sit with everyone and pick at their food, scooting it around on their plate, not eating much. Then an hour later I'll find them out back, digging around for that same food in the garbage."

I shook my head, hardly able to believe it.

"Why would they do that," I asked, "when they have a perfectly good meal in front of them?"

"I'm not certain," said Cindy, "but I know it's awfully hard for them to drop the homeless lifestyle. It becomes who they are, and they don't believe they're worth anything more. They do the same thing with bathing."

"What do you mean?" I asked.

"Well, you get the people off the streets and in the house, and they don't want to bathe. It takes most of them days, sometimes weeks, before they'll shower."

Cindy and I chatted for a few more minutes and exchanged numbers. I then made my way to the front of the room for the close of the conference.

As the worship team played, our conversation played on repeat in my mind. As I looked out at the sea of women, I wondered to myself, *How many of us do the same thing, spiritually?*

The last part of the conference was our closing remarks. Each of the speakers was asked to share what she most wanted the attendees to take with them. I shared what Cindy had told me, and related it to our journey with God.

If you are a follower of Christ, you are invited to the banquet. He lays before you a feast. The feast represents life in Him. The dumpster represents life before.

Jesus beckons you to a better way. It's the narrow way, the path less taken. It is the way of the righteous, the way of the courageous. It is for those who swim upstream, those who fight against the crowd, who aren't swayed by deceitful tongues or lying lips.

His is the way of honesty, the way of truth, the way of freedom.

By the blood of Christ, you are free. The shackles of bondage are broken. Sin has no hold on you and death has no power over you.

If He is your Lord, then you have tasted the sweet nectar of mercy. You don't need to drink the bitter gall of shame. He has wiped your slate clean; your record is spotless. He has cloaked you in forgiveness and sealed you with His Spirit. Don't go digging in the garbage for your mistakes. He has cast your sin as far as the east is from the west and hurled all your transgressions into the depths of the sea.

He knows the long list of offenses against you; He knows the names of those who hurt you. He knows exactly who you are and everything you've done.

In Him is an offer of rest, an invitation to set the burden down. Your shoulders weren't built to bear the weight of that yoke. Don't let anger, resentment, and unforgiveness chain you to the past.

You are free, but there is no freedom apart from Him. And there is no knowledge of Him apart from His Word.

Open His Word, and let the breath of the Spirit blow across your face. Write His Word on your heart and hear Him speak. Walk with Him through the Garden. Stroll with Him along the shores of the Sea of Galilee. Eat dinner beside Him near the crackling fire.

He sets before you the choicest foods and the best wine, milk, honey, and living water. He is the Bread of Life who drank the cup of wrath due us and offers us the cup of salvation so that we might live.

Don't have an encounter with Christ and walk away unmarked. Pray He might ruin you for lesser things. Let Him wreak havoc on your soul. Don't refuse the cleansing—let the conviction of the Spirit have its way with you, excising the tumorous roots of bitterness, unforgiveness, and anger. Let the Living Water wash away your stains.

The Lord has set before you a banquet, and you are a child of the King.

Pull up a chair and stay awhile, or an eternity. Open wide your mouth, and He will fill it with good things.[20]

Don't go back to the dumpster. Don't go back to the chains. It is for freedom that Christ set you free, and if the Son sets you free, you are free indeed.

The Lord of Lords and King of Kings has ransomed us for Kingdom things. Let's recline at the table and eat like it.

> Jesus said, "Have the people sit down." There was plenty of grass in that place, and they sat down (about five thousand men were there). Jesus then took the loaves, gave thanks, and distributed to those who were seated as much as they wanted. He did the same with the fish. When they had all had enough to eat, he said to his disciples, "Gather the pieces that are left over. Let nothing be wasted." So they gathered them and filled twelve baskets with the pieces of the five barley loaves left over by those who had eaten.
>
> —John 6:10 –13

---

20 Psalm 81:10

THE GOD OF "HERE-AND-NO-FURTHER"

> She gave this name to the LORD who spoke to her: "You are the God who sees me," for she said, "I have now seen the One who sees me."
>
> —Genesis 16:13

Pulitzer Prize-winning author and columnist Thomas L. Friedman once said, "In the world of ideas, to name something is to own it."[21] If you can name an issue, you can own the issue.

A provocative thought, and one that surfaces in Bible study. Throughout the pages of Scripture, particularly the Old Testament, when an individual comes face-to-face with the sovereignty of God, they name Him.

Of course, you and I know you can't name or own the Great I Am, but there is a point in the life of the believer when you move from *believing in* to *surrendering to*. It is then and only then that God becomes your God.

In Genesis 16:13 Hagar calls God *El-Roi*, the God who sees. In Genesis 22:14 Abraham says *Jehovah Jireh* (the LORD who provides) after God provided a substitutionary ram as a sacrifice in place of Isaac, his son. And in Psalm 23, the most beloved of Psalms, David uses the name *Jehovah Rohi,* or "the Lord is my Shepherd."

If I were to give God a name, He would be the "God of Here-and-

---

21 Thomas L. Friedman, "The Power of Green," The New York Times Magazine, (April 15th, 2007): Accessed April 11th, 2017, http://www.nytimes.com/2007/04/15/magazine/15green.t.html

No-Further."

The God I know, the God who has made His presence known to me every day of my recollected life, has always been the God of limits.

As a fifteen-year-old girl and again as a twenty-one-year-old woman, thoughts of suicide wove their way through my consciousness, whispering words of sweet relief to my tormented mind.

"*NO*," said the Lord. And while I might've allowed the drama to unfold in my imagination, the God of Here-and-No-Further kept me safe from myself. Time and time again through my tumultuous teens and early twenties, He let me peer over the cliff, but never tumble off of it.

At the age of thirty-five, I saw the God of Here-and-No-Further again, this time in my car. I was an alcoholic, desperate to quit and terrified to try. I was on a dangerous road, and I knew it. The Lord allowed me to see a glimpse of my destination, the possibility of a lost job and a ruined marriage. Then He allowed me to feel the weight of His love. He beckoned me to follow His voice. I made a choice that wasn't really a choice at all and rededicated my life to Christ.

Five years went by peacefully, for the most part, save the usual bumps and bruises of life.

Then, the God of Here-and-No-Further inserted Himself, once again, into a pain buried so deep I scarcely knew it was there.

First, the Ray Rice controversy: Video surfaced of the Baltimore Ravens running back punching his wife in the face then dragging her limp body into a hotel hallway and abandoning her like a sack of old clothes.

Naturally, we talked about it on the radio.

Then, the question: "You were in an abusive relationship too, once, right?" asked my co-host, shortly before we went on. I nodded. Not knowing the firestorm it would ignite inside me, he pressed on. "Can we talk about it on-air?"

A gulp, a brave smile, and a forced, "Of course!"

So I dug up a chunk of my life that I'd just as soon erase. In my early twenties, I was involved with one of those guys. A smooth-talking manipulator who knew just what to say and just when to say it. But did it ever cross the line into abuse?

Well, he certainly took advantage of me, but I let him, right?

And he was oh-so-good at taking what I thought was a valid complaint and spinning it around so fast that before I knew what had hit me, I was the one crying and asking for forgiveness.

And there was that time, or maybe it was twice, that I wore long sleeves to hide the finger-shaped bruises on my arms.

So we talked about it. And that was that.

Or so I thought.

The Sunday following the conversation, a woman stopped me in the hallway of our church.

"My husband heard you sharing your story on the air the other day," she said. "Thank you so much for being brave enough to talk about it! I know you are helping so many women."

I have to confess I had no idea what she was talking about. I have a multi-faceted testimony. Anytime someone asks me to share my story I laugh to myself and ask, "Which one?" Shall we talk about the eating disorder or the alcoholism? How about my years and years of people-pleasing or the time I made up a fake name to post a comment on someone's blog and then called them to confess it?

But suddenly it hit me.

Oh. *That* story.

And something inside me shut down. I smiled at the woman, thanked her for the encouragement, and raced off. I pushed the thoughts back down to their proper place and went to Sunday school.

Sunday night the thoughts came back.

Out of nowhere a memory burst in uninvited as I was drifting off to sleep, and suddenly it was sixteen years ago, and I was afraid. *No*, I thought to myself and directed my thoughts to other things. But this time it wouldn't go away.

Please, Lord, I prayed, *I don't want to think about this!*

But my God is the God of Here-and-No-Further, and He was not going to let this one die.

Remember it, He insisted, so I did. I remembered every painful detail. Every word shouted. Every horrible, humiliating thing. Every emotion I felt and every tear I cried. And I felt Him say, *Now verbalize it. What are you feeling?*

Rejection.

There, I said it. The word I had avoided for years. *Rejection.* Though he had threatened to kill himself if I left, when I finally did, he didn't stop me. He never even tried.

I had given him everything—the very best I had to offer, and it was not enough. I could not make him happy, and I could not make him love me the way I wanted him to.

Completely, thoroughly, utterly rejected.

Then the God of Here-and-No-Further interrupted. And if you have suffered the pain of divorce, or if your friends have turned on you, or you lost the promotion to someone else, you need to hear what He said to me.

You are *not* rejected. On the contrary my friend, you have been *selected.* Isaiah the prophet declared this to God's people: "I took you from the ends of the earth, from its farthest corners I called you. I said, 'You are my servant; *I have chosen you and have not rejected you.*'"[22]

As I lay in bed that night, God reminded me that the One who spoke the universe into being is also the One who hardens and softens hearts. He opens and closes doors. He can use rejection as a tool and will purpose it to achieve His purposes when it pleases Him.

You. Were. Not. Rejected.

Not rejected, so stop living dejected, and start living *selected.*

> For He chose us in Him before the creation of the world to be holy and blameless in His sight. In love He predestined us for adoption to sonship through Jesus Christ, in accordance with His pleasure and will, to the praise of His glorious grace, which He has freely given us in the One He loves.
>
> —Ephesians 1:4–5

God created you on purpose, with purpose, to live purposefully. He created you to do more than you could imagine or conceive of and will use rejection to prune you, protect you, and direct you.

---

22 Isaiah 41:9 (emphasis mine).

What if I had stayed?

I would have missed out on the love of my life. God selected me to be the wife of Mike, and the mother to my two children, Caitlyn and Nick. I would have missed out on the blessings of living near my parents in the great state of Texas and a radio career in Dallas/Fort Worth. I might have missed out on my ministry.

Someone once said your greatest pain is often the launching pad to your destiny. I don't know if that's true, but I do know that God has used every second of my past to allow me to minister to others in my present. And the more I minister to others, the more grateful I am for my past.

As I finally found sleep that night, I imagined myself holding my tattered heart out to Jesus. As He touched it, it became brand new—better than before—filled to the measure with Him and ready to pour love into the hearts of others.

When I woke up, I felt lighter. Not rejected, but selected. No longer walking dejected, but with my head held high.

Perhaps the God of Here-and-No-Further wants to be that same God to you. Perhaps He won't let you walk forward until you allow Him to heal the old wounds of the past. Walking in dejection, carrying old rejection, tethers us to the pain of years-gone-by. His is the heart of a pastor, the heart of a father and a mother. His delight is to set the captives free.

> I, the Lord, have called you in righteousness; I will take hold of your hand. I will keep you and will make you to be a covenant for the people and a light for the Gentiles, to open eyes that are blind, to free captives from prison and to release from the dungeon those who sit in darkness.
>
> —Isaiah 42:6–7

MUSCLE WRESTLE GONE AWRY

What songs make up the playlist to the soundtrack of your life?

"Danger Zone" by Kenny Loggins takes me back to fall 1987 when Sarah-something-or-other and I made up a dance in gym class. Anything by Toad the Wet Sprocket and I'm in college again. Summer '96 is forever marked by "There's Your Trouble" by the Dixie Chicks.

Summer 2014 was the summer of Rocky.

I introduced my seven-year-old son to *Rocky III* one night when my husband and daughter were out. My father took me to see it in the theater in 1982—Rocky Balboa vs. Clubber Lang. I can quote almost every line. Survivor's "Eye of the Tiger" floods me with a strange surge of determination, and a stranger urge to box.

Hi, my name is Rebecca, and I'm a Rocky-aholic.

At least, I was.

The torch has officially passed to Nick.

We finished *Rocky III*, had a brief discussion on the wisdom of renting another movie when we had to get up early the next day, threw caution to the wind, and started *Rocky IV.*

And so the floodgates were opened.

The next morning Mike and I awoke to the faint but familiar strains of the Rocky theme song. Nick, rising before anyone else, had successfully navigated the complicated system of Verizon's On-Demand service and rented the first installment of the series.

Then we watched the second. And the third, again. And the fourth, again. Our family has now seen each movie more times than we can count, and my husband and I have spent countless evenings shaking our heads, watching our son shadowbox in front of the television.

Enter *Muscle Wrestle*.

Muscle Wrestle is precisely what you might imagine. Or maybe not. The game went like this: Each night after dinner, Nick suited up, complete with boxing gloves and mouth guard. Caitlyn and I took our spots in the hallway, started the Rocky theme song (yes, I'm serious), and clapped and cheered as Nick pounded on his father, hollering phrases like "Dead meat," and "You ain't so bad!"

And Mike, the good dad that he is, took it like a champ, breaking away every so often for the occasional body slam or head lock while Nick shrieked with delight.

Muscle Wrestle was my favorite part of the day.

Some may think it's too violent. I thought it was awesome. Quality time has always been Nick's love language, and boys show affection through aggression. I am very much for Muscle Wrestle when it's authorized and supervised.

One evening, it wasn't.

Mike and I had chastised the kids several times for roughhousing. After clearing the table I went upstairs, leaving Caitlyn and Nick with their *final warning*: "If I have to come down here again both of you are going to your rooms for the night!"

Fifteen minutes later a crash followed by a scream brought my nighttime routine to a screeching halt.

"Mommm-mmmmy!"

Mike and I nearly ran each other over in our race to see what had happened.

The scene that met us was grim: two crying children, one shattered lamp. Not just any old lamp—the three-foot crystal lamp that my ninety-six-year-old grandmother had recently purchased for me.

After making sure the children were okay, I sent them upstairs while my husband surveyed the damage. His verdict? Beyond repair.

I felt sick. It's not that the lamp was priceless; it's that my grandmother wanted so much to buy it for me. Aware of her mortality, she had wanted to give me something that would remind me of her when she was gone.

As Mike and I cleaned up the broken glass, we discussed consequences and various ways the kids might pay for a new one. Then I remembered Six Flags.

We had made a deal with the kids at the beginning of summer; read twenty books with more than one chapter, and we'll take you to Six Flags. We had spent hours at the library choosing books, and each day the kids had one hour of quiet time when electronics went off and they retreated to their special spot to read. Nick had hit his twenty just that week, and Caitlyn was only a book or two away.

With my mind made up, I climbed the stairs and made my way down the hall to their bedrooms.

I sat them down on Nick's bed and looked at my children. Two frightened, tear-stained faces looked back at me, and my heart melted.

I knelt in front of them and told them I knew they hadn't broken the lamp on purpose. I accepted their apologies and reassured them of my love. Then I laid out the consequences.

"Caitlyn, Nick, I am upset about the lamp. Great-grandma Williams bought it for me and it was special to me. But I am more upset that you disobeyed me. Daddy and I had already asked you *three times* to stop playing Muscle Wrestle. And because you wouldn't listen, my lamp is broken."

"Can't Daddy fix it?"

"Not this time, Nick. So you and Caitlyn need to replace it."

"Okay, Mommy. I have twenty dollars from my report card money."

"Caitlyn, I'm afraid it costs more than twenty dollars. In fact, Daddy and I figured out that the cost of the lamp is the same amount of money it takes for our family to spend a day at Six Flags. So instead of going to Six Flags this summer, you two are going to buy me the lamp."

Nick immediately burst into tears, howling, "That's not fair! I read the books! I read all twenty of my books!"

Caitlyn, on the other hand, with tears streaming down her face, whispered, "Okay, Mommy."

Oh, how my heart ached. We had been planning the trip for months, watching videos of the Titan online and debating over which ride was the scariest. To take this away from them went against every natural instinct I have and made me physically sick to my stomach.

But we had to do it. What an injustice to my children, to let the incident go unpunished, thereby teaching them they could do what they wanted when they wanted with little to no repercussions. Better by far they learn the hard lessons when the risk is low and the cost is minimal—when you break other people's things, you replace them.

An hour later, my daughter tiptoed into my room.

"Mommy?"

"Yes, sweetheart?"

"I made you something."

She placed a card on my dresser and left.

"Dear Mommy, I am very very very very very very very very very very very sorry. I am so so so so so so so sorry. It's okay if you don't love me anymore. I know you don't forgive me because I don't forgive my-self. I hate myself, and God hates me too. Love, Caitlyn."

No way. No way was I going to allow my sweet, sensitive, tender-hearted daughter to heap burning coals of shame on her head.

I knocked on her door.

"Caitlyn?"

My daughter was under the covers, sobbing quietly.

"Sweetheart, honey, come here. Let Mommy hold you."

For a while we sat like that—me, rocking her gently as she cried. Then I tilted her head up, wiped her tears, and kissed her face.

"Sweet girl, let me ask you a question. Do you think it surprises me when you and Nick break things?"

A sniff, an eye wipe, and a head nod.

"Oh no, no, no. Let me tell you something. When Daddy and I de-cided to be parents, we knew exactly what we were getting in to. We knew, at some point, you and your brother would make big messes, color on the walls, and break stuff. I have never, at any point in being your mommy, expected you to be perfect."

A faint glimmer of hope flashed across her face.

"I make mistakes all the time, honey. I know you are going to make many mistakes in your life, and it is my job to teach you how to be re-sponsible for your mistakes. When you break something that belongs to somebody, you have to replace it. I wouldn't be a very good mommy if I didn't teach you that."

A sniffle, followed by a slight nod.

"So, Caitlyn, I need you to understand that I am not angry at you. And you could break a million lamps, and I would still love you. You could break a *trillion* lamps, and I would still forgive you. And there is nothing, *nothing* that you could do that would make God stop loving you. You are not big enough or powerful enough to make Him ever stop loving you."

We spent the next half hour snuggling, talking about fun free things we could do instead of Six Flags. Finally, exhausted from crying, my daughter fell asleep.

Have you done something you can't let go of? There is something you need to know about your Heavenly Father.

> Then the Lord came down in the cloud and stood there with him and proclaimed his name, the Lord. And he passed in front of Moses, proclaiming, "The Lord, the Lord, the compassionate and gracious God, slow to anger, abounding in love and faithfulness, maintaining love to thousands, and forgiving wickedness, rebellion and sin. Yet he does not leave the guilty unpunished; he punishes the children and their children for the sin of the parents to the third and fourth generation."
>
> —Exodus 34:6–7

The very first attribute of Himself that He lists is compassion. Not justice, not judgment, not holiness, but compassion. Can I tell you what makes this passage so remarkable? Only a mere two chapters earlier in the book of Exodus, the Israelites, weary of waiting for Moses to come down from Mount Sinai, had taken their gold, melted it down, created a calf, and worshiped it.

And what does God want Moses to know about Himself? That He is a God of compassion, extending grace to the undeserving and remaining patient in the midst of their waywardness. His love and faithfulness extend to generation upon generation, and His forgiveness is as vast as the heavens.

But what about the children of the guilty? Does He punish sons and daughters for the sins of their fathers and mothers? Should I punish my future grandchildren for breaking my grandmother's lamp? No. The New American Commentary suggests the following:

> This wording means something quite different from what it might seem to mean to the casual reader. It does not mean that God would punish children and grandchildren for something their ancestors did but that they themselves did not do. Rather, it describes God's just punishment of a given type of sin in each new generation as that sin continues to be repeated down through the generations.[23]

Our Heavenly Father, your God, and mine, races toward the repentant like the father raced toward his prodigal son. As Douglas Stuart so eloquently states, "He does not reluctantly forgive sins against himself and others; he does so eagerly, as a manifestation of his character, by which he delights in doing so."[24]

We did not go to Six Flags that summer. Holding my ground was one of the harder things I've had to do as a parent, but it was the loving thing to do.

Did I forgive my kids?

Instantly. No doubt about it. Not even a question.

Did I extend grace?

Oceans of it.

Compassion?

By the boatload.

There is now no condemnation for those who live in the Carrell house. Consequences, yes. But condemnation, never.

That goes for you too, you know. Perhaps you are sifting through the consequences of some of your own bad choices. Not one of them surprised God. He knew what He was getting into with you when He purchased your salvation through the blood of His Son, and He has no buyer's remorse. He knew you would fall and fail and He knows your

---

23 D. K. Stuart, *Exodus, vol. 2* (Nashville: Broadman & Holman Publishers, 2006), 717 (brackets mine).
24 Ibid, 216.

current struggle with sin. Know this: Your Heavenly Father stubbornly refuses to condemn you. He stubbornly insists on bestowing mercy
to you. And He will never, not ever, no matter what, stop loving you.

> Who is a God like you,
> who pardons sin and forgives the transgression
> of the remnant of his inheritance?
> You do not stay angry forever
> but delight to show mercy.
> You will again have compassion on us;
> you will tread our sins underfoot
> and hurl all our iniquities into the depths of the sea.
> —Micah 7:18–19

THE TEN-DOLLAR BILL

One person gives freely, yet gains even more; another with-holds unduly, but comes to poverty. A generous person will prosper; whoever refreshes others will be refreshed.

—Proverbs 11:24–25 NIV

A friend of mine turned me on to the concept several years ago, but I'd never tried it for myself until fall 2016.

Praying for one word.

The idea is simple and best described by Mike Ashcraft, author of the bestselling book *My One Word*.

> The concept of My One Word is simple. Lose the long list of resolutions—all your sweeping promises to change—and do something about one thing this year instead of nothing about everything. Choose just one word that represents what you most hope God will do in you, and focus on it for an entire year. This single act will force clarity and con-centrate your efforts. As you focus on your word over an extended period of time, you position yourself for God to form your character at a deep, sustainable level. Growth and change will result.[25]

My friend Debbie has been implementing the "one-word" practice since the book came out in 2012. Last year her word was "sacrifice."

---

25 Mike Ashcroft and Rachel Olsen, *My One Word* (Grand Rapids: Zondervan, 2008), 2012.

Sacrifice, I thought to myself as she filled me in. Nope. No, thank you. Not for me.

Until I decided to do it.

The word I got was "prayer."

In late fall 2016 I started to feel some spiritual unrest. I sensed the Lord prompting me to spend more time in focused, concentrated prayer.

I have kept a prayer journal since the eighth grade. I have no memories that do not include the Lord, and I have been talking to Him in my head since the time I could talk. But I sensed that He desired more.

I began to make more of an effort on my long quiet drive into the office each day around 4:00 a.m. The only problem was that I'd get distracted, or dazed, or start thinking about dinner.

So I decided to pray out loud.

One morning I asked the Lord to help me pray. I wanted to pray with power and intention, without wandering thoughts. I wanted to pray the prayers He wanted me to pray.

By the time I made it to downtown Dallas I was praying out loud, in the name of Jesus, hand in the air like you just don't care. And the strangest thing happened.

A picture of a ten-dollar bill flitted across my mind.

I knew this ten-dollar bill. It was the one sitting in my wallet. The one earmarked for Chick-fil-A. The one that tantalizingly promised a grilled chicken cool wrap with fries and a drink.

"It's yours, Lord," I said aloud in my car. "Who can I bless today? Who needs help?"

Downtown Dallas, like any big city, has a large homeless population. It's not uncommon to see a man or woman asleep on a bench or sitting listlessly against a building. As I made my way slowly down the road, I scanned up and down the streets, straining my eyes to catch a glimpse of someone I could help.

Nothing.

Stopping at an intersection, I looked around hopefully.

No one.

I sighed with disappointment. Well, maybe I would have Chick-fil-A after all.

Then I saw him. A tall man, walking my way with his head down. He was wearing a winter coat and looked clean-shaven—not the homeless person I'd been looking for.

He shuffled across the street in front of my car as I waited on the edge of my seat. *Was this him? Did he need help? What are we doing, Lord?*

All of the sudden he turned and looked me square in the eyes. I smiled my best "How Can I Help You Today" smile and to my surprise, he smiled back. He paused before he continued walking and I sensed that he was struggling with whether or not to ask me something.

I was right.

"Um, miss?"

I rolled down my window. "Hi," I said. "Can I help you?"

"Oh, no. Well, I am on my way to catch the train, and I don't have quite enough money. Is there any way you could spare some change?"

Is there any way—are you kidding me?

And then, like a lunatic, I opened my mouth.

"Oh my goodness! You're not going to believe this. I was driving down to work—I live in Flower Mound. So I was driving and praying, and God put it on my heart to bless someone with the money I had in my wallet, so, yes, I can help you!"

Wisely, he backed up a step from the crazy lady.

It didn't stop me.

"Seriously, you're not going to believe this! God wants you to have this ten-dollar bill. I have been looking for the person I was going to give it to, and it's you!"

We chatted through another red light cycle, and he was on his way. His parting words will stay with me forever.

"You have no idea how much I needed this. God picked the right person for you to bless! You just have no idea!"

I think maybe I do.

I'm not a prophet, and I don't claim to have any special revelation from God, but here is what I sense: The blessing had very little to do with a silly ten-dollar bill, and everything to do with realizing that God sees him.

That moment was a miracle.

Would it have happened if I hadn't prayed? I have no doubts.

That man was still going to cross that street. I doubt I would've smiled at him, had I not been looking for him, and he may or may not have asked me for spare change. If he had, I still would have given him the ten-dollar bill.

But I would've done it begrudgingly, not joyfully.

Out of guilt-motivated obedience instead of Spirit-driven mission.

I would've been irritated at the loss of Chick-fil-A instead of gaining a miraculous moment with the Lord.

And the man, while making his train, would've missed the blessing of knowing that God was truly looking out for him, even when He seemed far away.

It was a miracle because, in my prayer, God bent my will to His, and used me for His purpose.

Can I tell you something?

I wouldn't trade that moment for a lifetime of Chick-fil-A.

My word for 2017 is prayer, but I didn't understand why until that day.

A life of consistent, intentional prayer is a life of power, excitement, and exhilaration. God speaks to us in the Bible and works through us in our prayers. Prayer is where we get swept up into the sovereign will of the Creator of the Universe. It is where He shifts our perspective and broadens our understanding. It is the conduit through which His power flows, through which we receive His grace, strength, and love.

I am convinced that prayer is what moves us from natural to supernatural, from ordinary to extraordinary, and from mediocrity to a life lived on mission.

The one-word concept, according to Ashcroft, positions us before God so that He can form our "character at a deep, substantial level."

I wonder what the church would look like if we lived under the banner of prayer.

> For this reason, ever since I heard about your faith in the Lord Jesus and your love for all God's people, I have not stopped giving thanks for you, remembering you in my prayers. I keep asking that the God of our Lord Jesus Christ,

the glorious Father, may give you the Spirit of wisdom and revelation, so that you may know him better. I pray that the eyes of your heart may be enlightened in order that you may know the hope to which he has called you, the riches of his glorious inheritance in his holy people, and his incomparably great power for us who believe. That power is the same as the mighty strength he exerted when he raised Christ from the dead and seated him at his right hand in the heavenly realms, far above all rule and authority, power and dominion, and every name that is invoked, not only in the present age but also in the one to come.

—Ephesians 1:15–20 NIV

THE COMPOST HEAP

I will refresh the weary and satisfy the faint.

—Jeremiah 31:25

Have these words ever described you?

Tired.

Uninspired.

Plodding along.

Going through the motions.

That description fit me like a well-tailored suit as I sat, listlessly, in the pew. Try as I might to focus on the pastor, my mind wouldn't pay attention, wandering from one thought to another, finally landing on what I needed to get at the grocery store later that day.

The congregation laughed, snapping me back to the present. I looked up at the screen, down at the open Bible in my lap, and smiled as though I was in on the joke.

At the end of the sermon, the band began to play, cueing the ushers to pass the plates. I closed my eyes and raised my hands, willing my heart to worship.

I suppose that day I looked the part: Church dress on, Bible in one hand, coffee in the other with two bright-eyed kids in tow.

On the inside, however, I was empty.

Welcome to the Dry Place.

That particular morning was one in a string of many days spent wandering and wondering—why was God silent? What had I done? What was wrong with me?

Ever been there?

Later that day I went for a run. For some reason, I sense God's Presence more when I'm outside, by myself, pounding the hot Texas pavement. If I need to hear from the Lord and all else has failed, I lace up my shoes and hit the road.

As I jogged, I wrestled with my thoughts and pleaded with the Lord to speak. I rewound the tapes of the past month's events, searching for clues that might explain my spiritual listlessness. Eventually, my mind drifted back to an interview I'd done with Lisa Williams, a friend of mine in Christian radio.

I'd known Lisa for about a year. We met at the KCBI studios when she got stuck in Dallas due to bad weather. North Texas is not known for its cold winters, and we seldom get snow, but once every five or six years we'll get hit with what meteorologists call "an ice event."

That year it was more like icemageddon.

Unable to catch a flight, she (nervously) took a cab to our offices to catch up with our general manager, Matt Austin, whom she's known for years.

We connected instantly, so a few months later when Lisa asked me to talk openly about my history with alcohol abuse and bulimia, I agreed.

Perhaps it was because I was so comfortable with my friend, but I went deeper into the ugly details than I ever had publicly. And while it felt freeing at the time, I must confess I had some sharer's remorse in the days following.

As I ran, it began to make sense. Combing through my tangled past opened up some unresolved shame and guilt. In sharing my secrets, I'd been forced to pry open a door I'd rather keep shut. In a very real sense, it was as though I'd opened up an old dumpster and waded through decades-old trash. Although I exited the dumpster quickly, the stench had not gone away.

I cried out to the Lord for forgiveness.

Again.

And instead of feeling peace, a picture of my compost heap flashed in my mind.

I pushed the thought aside and went back to confessing.

Again.

This time I heard the stern, soft whisper of the Lord.

If we confess our sins, He is faithful and righteous to forgive us our sins and to cleanse us from all unrighteousness.

—1 John 1:9 NASB

In Christ's economy, a sin confessed is a sin forgiven. Psalm 103:12 states that when we turn and repent from our transgressions God casts them as far as the east is from the west. The prophet Isaiah declared that the Lord hides our rebellious acts behind His back,[26] never to remember them again.[27] Micah reminded the Israelites that God is compassionate toward His people, delighting in showing them mercy and hurling their iniquities into the depths of the sea.

Out there on the road by myself, the Holy Spirit gently chided me to lose the scuba gear and stop deep sea fishing.

What would you say if I told you that to reconfess the same old stuff over and over is to deny the finishing power of the cross?

As I turned this over in my mind, the picture of my compost heap broke through my thoughts again.

What? What, Lord? I asked myself. *Why are You showing me my compost dump?*

Although I don't garden, I have been composting our organic trash for three years in hopes that someday I might sprout a green thumb.

That's when it hit me.

I had taken another load of trash outside just the other day and had been delighted to see that I had all kinds of things sprouting up: green onions, a sweet-potato vine, even an avocado plant. We go through a lot of vegetables each week, and in the rich soil of our waste, the remains were growing and thriving.

"See?" whispered the Lord to my hurting heart, "I grow beautiful things out of the garbage of your life."

The floodgates opened as tears cascaded down my cheeks, ending my spiritual drought.

---

26 Isaiah 38:17
27 Isaiah 43:25

It was true. If I didn't have a past, would I have a testimony? If I hadn't strayed so far, would I be as bold to proclaim the prodigal chasing nature of our God? Surely if I hadn't swum in shame, grace would not be so sweet. The reason I'd entered the ministry in the first place was that I wanted others to know the saving power of our Savior; a power I knew from first-hand experience.

I have yet to meet a man or a woman that wouldn't rewrite pages and even chapters of their history. While I wish my story were one of joyful obedience from the beginning, I know that our faith is showcased through our repentance, and God's glory is displayed as He transforms us one day at a time.

Our Heavenly Father is faithful to redeem our mistakes and repurpose our past when we place our hope in His hands. So the next time you're tempted to dumpster dive remember this and rejoice:

God grows beautiful things out of the garbage of our lives.

But if we walk in the Light as He Himself is in the Light, we have fellowship with one another, and the blood of Jesus His Son cleanses us from all sin. If we say that we have no sin, we are deceiving ourselves and the truth is not in us. If we confess our sins, He is faithful and righteous to forgive us our sins and to cleanse us from all unrighteousness.

—1 John 1:7–9

THE MAMMOGRAM

The LORD God made garments of skin for Adam and his wife, and clothed them.

—Genesis 3:21

I stared at myself in the mirror of the empty changing room. It was eerily silent; the only sound was my heart beating angrily against the wall of my chest.

I had put it off for over two years. I would've put it off longer if I hadn't met Jan Greenwood.

Jan serves as the Equip Pastor at Gateway Church, a megachurch in Southlake, Texas, that boasts a congregation of over twenty thousand members. Before that, she had been the women's pastor for roughly a decade.

Jan has overcome stage four breast cancer.

Twice.

Her book "Women at War" opens with the story of her first diagnosis. She went to the doctor for pain in her hips and legs. What they found was cancer in her breasts that had metastasized to her bones.

She joined us on the air on *Mornings With Jeff and Rebecca* with one clear message:

Don't put off your mammogram!

Done.

What must have been minutes felt like forever as I stood there, freezing, in a scratchy paper gown that opened in the front. As the seconds ticked by my anxiety mounted, and I tried to talk myself down.

Breast cancer doesn't run in our family. Cousin Kathy was a cousin by marriage. Her story isn't your story. Your health is in the Lord's hands.

"Ms. Carrell?"

I whipped around, startled, as the petite pixie-eyed mammo technician poked her head in the door. She looked like a senior in high school fresh from cheerleading practice. The last thing in the world I wanted to do was disrobe in front of this blond-haired, doe-eyed Southern belle, but I put on my best fake smile and, well, faked it.

"Right this way," she chirped.

I followed her down a long hallway (at least it feels long when you're wearing construction paper) and through a large steel door.

"Is this your first time?" she asked.

"Yep. Yes, it is," I said, laughing awkwardly.

"And you're forty-two?"

Sigh. "Turning forty-three in May."

She looked up from her notes, the corners of her cherry-blossom mouth turned down. "You really shouldn't put off your mammogram, Ms. Carrell. Your chart says you have a cousin who had stage four breast cancer?"

"Yes. Well, not a blood cousin. I mean, she's a cousin through marriage. On my dad's side."

She looked back down at her notes.

"Okay, then!" she exclaimed, sounding far more enthusiastic than the situation warranted. "Let's get started."

I will spare you the gory details. Suffice it to say I had never been stretched, pulled, and squished so much in my life. Painful? No. Uncomfortable? Not bad. What caught me by surprise was the shame.

I can't remember the last time I'd felt so exposed.

I go for my check-up every year. I've had two kids. It's not like I've never had to disrobe, but this, for some reason, was different.

As I stood there while the sweet young technician contorted my arms every which way, all I wanted to do was hide. The flimsy paper shirt-dress lay crumpled on the chair. The tech was oblivious, stretching and pulling and telling me not to breathe.

Finally, it was over.

"You did great," she exclaimed, further supporting my cheerleader hypothesis. "That wasn't bad at all, was it?"

I tried unsuccessfully to match her enthusiasm but only squeaked out, "Nope!"

"Now, I need to warn you," she began.

Instantly she had my undivided attention. "Need to warn you" are not necessarily the words you are hoping to hear at your first mammogram.

"You have very dense breast tissue," she continued, "so don't be surprised if you get a callback."

My mind slipped back to my own high school years. I was sixteen years old, waiting outside the choir room for the theater director to post the call-back list after the spring musical tryouts.

This was a different callback.

"Come here; I'll show you," she said.

She pulled up the images, and while I didn't know what to look for, I did see what she meant. The tissue inside my breasts was thick and fibrous, showing up white on the X-ray film.

"It's hard to see inside, so your doctor may want to send you back for a 3-D mammogram. Those are really cool!"

I forced a smile, thanked her, and went back to my changing room.

On the way home, I thought about the experience.

Did you know that there has never been a society in recorded history that has not worn clothes? Modesty varies depending on the region, and some tribal groups wear less than we'd be comfortable with, but there has never been a culture that has not covered up.

Theologian Dr. R.C. Sproul, in an article on *Ligonier Ministries*, says, "The very first psychological self-awareness of guilt and shame was an uncomfortable awareness of nudity. Since then, human beings have been the only creatures who have adorned and covered themselves with artificial garments, because it is built into our fallen humanity to equate shame and humiliation with nakedness."[28]

The correlation of shame and nudity finds its origins in the Garden of Eden. In Genesis 2:25 we read that the man and woman were na-

---

28 Sproul, R.C., "Nakedness Equals Shame," *Ligonier Ministries*, January 9, 2015, accessed March 10, 2017, http://www.ligonier.org/blog/nakedness-equals-shame/.

ked, and the author seems to go out of his way to state "they felt no shame."

Seven verses later, after Eve and Adam eat the fruit of the tree of knowledge of good and evil, "they realized they were naked; so they sewed fig leaves together and made coverings for themselves."[29]

Sin stained their innocence, guilt clouded their thoughts, and in their shame, they hid. First from each other, covering skin with fig leaves, and then from God.

Some read the Garden account and the fall of mankind with a heavy sadness. When I read it, I find it dripping with hope.

The penalty for their sin was death, but God, in His mercy, established a plan to reconcile His people back to Himself. One day there would be an offspring, and the offspring of the woman would crush the head of the serpent.

Then He did the most curious thing.

He clothed them.

The LORD God looked on the man and woman with eyes of compassion. He saw their feeble attempts to cover themselves, and He did them one better.

He killed an animal, skinned it, and tenderly concealed their nakedness. What an act of love! Such grace bestowed on the original sinners, sacrificing an innocent animal to cover the sin of His children.

What started in the Garden continues today. Sproul says, "The only way any of us can stand in God's presence is to be stripped of those rags and then clothed afresh in the garments of Christ's righteousness. That is the Gospel. You and I can never stand in the presence of a holy God unless we are clothed from on high with a righteousness that is not our own."[30]

God still looks at us with eyes of compassion. Like the mammogram, He sees beyond the surface, all the way into the deepest crevices of our broken hearts. He sees the hurts we don't remember that cause the behavior we can't understand, and in His mercy, He drapes us in

---

29 Genesis 3:7
30 Sproul, "Nakedness Equals Shame."

robes of righteousness.

Is your past littered with mistakes and your present shrouded in shame? Sweet friend, your Savior has once and for all paid the price for your transgressions and cloaked you in the clothing of salvation. We can, as Paul exhorted the Ephesian believers, "Put off the old self which is being corrupted by its deceitful desires, be made new in the attitudes of your minds; and put on the new self, created to be like God in true righteousness and holiness."[31]

How do we do that?

By spending time with the object of our affections. It has been said "we become what we behold." The more time we spend with Christ in His Word, the more like Him we become. The longer we soak in the Gospel, the more real it becomes to us. As we gaze upon His face, allowing His light to heal our soul, the more natural it is to don the grace and forgiveness He offers.

Christ has given us a new set of clothes, far more effective than fig leaves or paper gowns. And our robes of righteousness are *stain resistant* to all who call Jesus "Lord."

> I am overwhelmed with joy in the Lord my God! For he has dressed me with the clothing of salvation and draped me in a robe of righteousness. I am like a bridegroom dressed for his wedding or a bride with her jewels.
>
> —Isaiah 61:10 NLT

---

31 Ephesians 4:22–24 NIV

A "MARY" LITTLE CHRISTMAS

But Martha was distracted by her many tasks, and she came up and asked, "Lord, don't You care that my sister has left me to serve alone? So tell her to give me a hand."

The Lord answered her, "Martha, Martha, you are worried and upset about many things, but one thing is necessary. Mary has made the right choice, and it will not be taken away from her."

—Luke 10:40–42 HCSB

Each year around the holidays, I usually receive a few invitations to share at various women's ministry events; invitations I accept eagerly and with deep gratitude.

I just love to talk about Jesus.

Honestly, He's my absolute favorite.

I start praying for the event well in advance, and those prayers usually go something like this:

So what do you want to talk about, Lord? Clock's ticking. Sure could use some insight.

There are the usual passages of Scripture preachers like to teach on around Christmas, like Isaiah 9:6, which states, "For unto us a child is born, unto us a Son is given, and the government will be on His shoulders, and He shall be called Wonderful Counselor, Mighty God, Eternal Father, Prince of Peace."

The Lukan narrative of Jesus' birth is another popular place to go, but this year, I couldn't tear myself away from the story of Mary and Martha.

The story is small, buried deep in the heart of the book of Luke, in the middle of our Savior's journey to Jerusalem, but it carries big implications for us that we can apply year round.

Luke's Gospel divides neatly into four sections, comprised of Jesus' birth and baptism (1:1—4:13), His ministry in Galilee (4:14—9:50), the journey to Jerusalem (9:51—19:44), and the Passion week leading to His crucifixion and resurrection (19:45—24:53). Each section has a theme, and the theme of the Jerusalem journey is this:

~ Jesus Offers a New Way ~

What is the new way? God the Father told Peter, James, and John when they were alone with Jesus on a mountaintop. "This is My Son, the Chosen One. Listen to Him."

~ Listen to Him ~

What God did in that simple statement was to turn the old way on its head—upside down and inside out. Backward front and front-wards back. A completely new way of approaching the God of Israel.

You see, the old way was about the "do."

It was about the "thou shalls" and "shall nots," the "cans" and "can nots," the "do's" and "do nots." It was about an ever-ascending ladder of laws that no man could hope to fulfill.

Ah, but that was the whole point.

The commands, the "thou shalls" and the "do's" were never meant to save the poor Israelites or anyone else. They were intended to show them how far they were from holiness, how great was their capacity to sin, and how desperately they needed a Savior.

The "do" was put in place to point us to a "Who."

~ The old way was about the Do. The new way is about the Who. ~

Martha learned that firsthand, late one afternoon, when a scraggly band of brothers came knocking at her door. They weren't strangers, far from it. Scripture indicates that Martha; her sister, Mary; and her brother, Lazarus, were dear friends of the rabbi they called Christ. In biblical times it was a great honor to offer your home to travelers and hospitality was expected.

Still, can we all just agree that Jesus and His disciples pulled a total "pop in"?

Maybe you keep your pantry stocked and your home pop-in ready, but as for me and my house, make a reservation.

Another thing that occurs to me is that in 30-or-so AD when this likely took place, there was not a kosher Kroger open twenty-four/ seven. A meal was a big deal. They made their flour. They butchered their cows. These things, I'm told, take time.

So I find it completely normal and natural that Martha would be scurrying around, scraping together a meal to feed at least thirteen hungry men. Martha, as a matter of fact, was doing *exactly* what Jewish society would have expected her to do.

Mary, on the other hand, was downright *scandalous*.

Women did not sit at the feet of teachers—that was the position of a disciple, and women were not disciples.

In fact, men would not talk to their wives in the public square, and neither would they walk next to them in the street. The women followed behind. Women were allowed no further in the temple than the outer court, along with the Gentiles.

Surely as the disciples watched the scene play out, they too, anticipated a scolding.

They got one, but not the one they expected.

How their eyes must've widened when Jesus, lovingly but firmly told Martha that she, not her sister, was in the wrong, and in fact, Mary had chosen the better thing.

Martha was still stuck in the old way, the way of the "do."

Sweet Mary, who anointed her Lord with oil and wiped His feet with her hair, who would watch in stunned silence when the Lord commanded her four-day-dead brother to stop being dead and come out of the tomb already, was all about the "Who."

She sat at His feet.

She leaned in.

She listened.

She chose the better thing, and it would not be taken from her.

And suddenly, what society said she should or shouldn't do didn't matter anymore, and neither did the world's expectations, because her Lord was in front of her and she was hanging on every single word.

At Dallas Seminary, we are taught to examine the text in a very-Mary-kind-of-way. I do think it's worth noting that Jesus did not correct Martha's busyness. He didn't scold her for serving or chasten her for huffing and puffing about her sister.

He ever so gently reprimanded the posture of her heart.

You see, the new way doesn't throw out the "do." The Bible is clear on this point.

- But be doers of the word, and not hearers only (James 1:22 HCSB).

- What good is it, my brothers, if someone says he has faith but does not have works? Can his faith save him (James 2:14)?

- And let us be concerned about one another in order to promote love and good works (Hebrews 10:24).

The new way changes the order of things. If we attempt the do without the Who we'll end up just like Martha, frustrated and grumpy that no one is helping.

The new way isn't a list; it's an invitation to spend time with our Lord in the Scriptures and wait on Him to speak. It's about leaning in and listening. It's choosing to live in a love that stepped off the throne, into skin, and climbed on a cross to bear our sin.

For Christians, every moment is a chance at a new start and a clean slate, because Jesus paid the penalty for our transgressions. My prayer for you, and myself, for that matter, is that we would live our lives in relationship with the "Who," and trust that He will tell us what to do.

> But your Teacher will not hide Himself any longer. Your eyes will see your Teacher, and whenever you turn to the right or to the left, your ears will hear this command behind you: "This is the way. Walk in it."
>
> —Isaiah 30:20b–21

WHEN WHIRLWINDS TALK

Then the LORD answered Job from the whirlwind.

—Job 38:1

Pain.

That is the word that comes to mind when I reflect on December 2016.

One friend struggled to smile as she spent her first Christmas without her father. Another drove five hours to memorialize her daddy after he died suddenly in a tragic accident. Another friend sat housebound, recovering from surgery after getting the unwelcome news that her thyroid had to go.

George Michael.

Carrie Fischer.

Debbie Reynolds.

An emotionally charged election that promised a heated and rocky transition into 2017.

Have you ever wanted to cry "Uncle?"

It seemed ironic that the book I was studying during this season was Job—the quintessential biblical book on suffering; one which, according to Daniel J. Estes, "probes the deepest theological and philosophical questions"[32] that mankind knows to ask.

Job was, as the author states, "a man of perfect integrity, who feared God and turned away from evil."[33] He lived in the period of the patri-

---

32 Daniel J. Estes, *Handbook on the Wisdom Books and Psalms* (Grand Rapids: Baker Academic, 2005), 24.
33 Job 1:1

archs and enjoyed the blessings of prosperity and a large family.

One day the angels, including Satan, were presenting themselves before the LORD. The text does not tell us why, but God's question to Satan suggests that the heavenly beings were giving an account of their whereabouts.

The LORD asked Satan, "Where have you come from?"

"From roaming the earth," Satan answered Him, "and walking around on it."

Then the LORD said to Satan, "Have you considered My servant Job? No one else on earth is like him, a man of perfect integrity, who fears God and turns away from evil."

Satan answered the LORD, "Does Job fear God for nothing? Haven't You placed a hedge around him, his household, and everything he owns? You have blessed the work of his hands, and his possessions have increased in the land. But stretch out Your hand and strike everything he owns, and he will surely curse You to Your face."

—Job 1:7–11

What follows is terrifying. God hands Job over to Satan's power and allows his servant to undergo trials and testing that trump any headline on the evening news.

Round one sees the loss of Job's servants, livestock, and children. Round two takes away his health, his appearance, and his dignity. Job is left only with a nagging wife and a few "frenemies" that gave their best counsel when they weren't speaking.

There are many rich and relevant lessons woven through this ancient literary work. Here are the three that rise to the top.

~ God meets us at the point of our deepest pain ~

The next thirty-five chapters paint vivid imagery of Job's anguish. His physical pain is surpassed only by his heartbreak. He insists on maintaining his innocence to Bildad, Zophar, and Eliphaz, who accuse him of the most heinous of crimes. He pleads for a hearing before the Almighty, only to meet silence from the LORD and ridicule from his "friends."

Finally, in the theophany of a whirlwind, Yahweh speaks.

A theophany is a physical manifestation of God, a phenomenon in which the Bible is replete. Remember the burning bush? That's a theophany.

Of all the forms God could have taken, how curious that He chose a whirlwind. Do you remember how Job's children died?

> He was still speaking when another messenger came and reported: "Your sons and daughters were eating and drinking wine in their oldest brother's house. Suddenly a powerful wind swept in from the desert and struck the four corners of the house. It collapsed on the young people so that they died, and I alone have escaped to tell you!"
>
> —Job 1:18–19

This powerful wind simultaneously struck all four corners of the house with such force that the dwelling was demolished along with everything and everyone inside of it. This was not a strong, straight-line wind; this was a whirlwind, likely caused when the warm desert air mixed with the cool, damp air blowing in off the Euphrates.

Why, then, would a loving God appear to Job in the very form that caused him such agonizing, ongoing grief?

Because God meets us in our deepest pain.

Psalm 27:5 says, "For in the day of trouble he will keep me safe in his dwelling; he will hide me in the shelter of his sacred tent and set me high upon a rock." When the moment you most fear arrives, and unless the LORD tarries, it will, He is faithful to surround you with His Presence and hide you in Himself. I have met many, many people who have suffered inconceivable loss. Those who know the LORD will attest that He met them at the point of their deepest pain.

~ God's silence is not to be mistaken for His absence ~

I am reminded of a time in my own life when I experienced the silence of God. I was going through a dry spell—feeling tired and uninspired. When I opened the Bible, it felt more like dead words on dry pages than alive and active. A friend of mine who teaches at an elementary school smiled and said, "Maybe you're in a test. The Teacher is always quiet during a test."

God still tests His children. He gave Satan permission to strike Job and sift Peter, and we have no scriptural indication that testing has ceased. Peter, speaking from firsthand experience, acknowledges that while we are tested, we are also protected.

> You are being protected by God's power through faith for a salvation that is ready to be revealed in the last time. You rejoice in this, though now for a short time you have had to struggle in various trials . . .

Don't miss what Peter is saying. He is not warning that trials might come. He is telling us in no uncertain terms that they will come because we must struggle.

Why?

Why would a loving God appoint times of testing and seasons of struggle?

> . . . so that the genuineness of your faith—more valuable gold, which perishes though refined by fire—may result in praise, glory, and honor at the revelation of Jesus Christ.
>
> —1 Peter 1:5–7

To test and prove that our faith is genuine because only genuine faith receives salvation.

This is the very question Job sought to understand, and while we have the advantage of knowing the heavenly dialogue that took place in chapters 1 and 2, Job never did. God never answered his question, but God was never absent. He emerges from hiding in chapter 38 with one clear message: *I am God, and you are not.* Which brings us to our last point.

~ We can rest in His sovereignty ~

Bible teacher and author Jen Wilkin and I spoke together at a conference in February 2017, and she gave this example:

> Hold your arms above your head and touch your hands together so that you make a big circle. Now imagine that, in that circle, is all of the knowledge there is to know. God is the author of knowledge, so He knows every single thing inside that circle. There is nothing to know that He does not know.
>
> Now imagine that there is a dot in the middle of the circle the size of the point of a safety pin. Cut the dot in half, then cut it in half again. That microscopic speck represents all of the knowledge that mankind can know. Inside that dot is everything that the most brilliant among us can know. The rest of us know about half of a half of that.

Her point was simple. If God knows all and we know little, who shall we trust when things go wrong?

Have you had to walk through the valley and wrestle with the unknown? Have you been hit with pain and suffering, and stumbled to your feet, only to get knocked down again?

You are not alone.

God is the God of the long game. He sits outside of time and sees the end from the beginning. Had Satan known how Job would respond, I think he'd have chosen someone else to mess with. But God knew exactly how Job would react.

Job remained faithful.

God also knew that Job's story would be pressed in the pages of Scripture, providing hope and comfort to millions through the millennia. Like an expert craftsman, He knew just how much pressure to apply—just how much pain to allow—before He pulled him from the fire and restored his body and spirit.

I will say to you what I said to my friends and what I often repeat to myself.

Your pain has an expiration date. Your problems, though real and painful, are temporary. My friend Melissa likes to say it this way, "You're in a life season, not a life sentence." And what does every season have in common?

A beginning, a middle, and an end.

Where you are now is not where you'll always be. Jesus promises that one day there will be "no more death, or mourning, or crying or pain,"[34] for He is making all things new.

Job was not privy to the drama unfolding in the heavenly realms. He had no idea that he was the rope in an epic battle of tug-o-war, but you and I have a different vantage point.

We know how the story ends. And because we know the end, we know we fight *from* victory, not *for* victory. We know that resurrection power dwells within us and propels us, equipping us to stand strong and persevere, even amidst pain and persecution.

We know that our Savior conquered the grave and we rest in the knowledge that one day soon, "every knee will bow and every tongue will confess that Jesus Christ is Lord.[35]"

So we wait. We pray. We fight. We stand tall and press on. We bear each other's burdens as we carry our crosses. And we look to the heavens, for our King is coming soon.

> Then I saw "a new heaven and a new earth," for the first heaven and the first earth had passed away, and there was no longer any sea. I saw the Holy City, the new Jerusalem, coming down out of heaven from God, prepared as a bride beautifully dressed for her husband. And I heard a loud voice from the throne saying, "Look! God's dwelling place is now among the people, and he will dwell with them. They will be his people, and God himself will be with them and be their God. 'He will wipe every tear from their eyes. There will be no more death' or mourning or crying or pain, for the old order of things has passed away."
>
> He who was seated on the throne said, "I am making everything new!" Then he said, "Write this down, for these words are trustworthy and true."

---

34 Revelation 21:4
35 Revelation 21:4

He said to me: "It is done. I am the Alpha and the Omega, the Beginning and the End. To the thirsty I will give water without cost from the spring of the water of life. Those who are victorious will inherit all this, and I will be their God and they will be my children.

—Revelation 21:1–7 NIV

THE HANDPRINT

The works of his hands are faithful and just; all his precepts
are trustworthy. They are steadfast for ever and ever, done
in faithfulness and uprightness. He provided redemption
for his people; he ordained his covenant forever —holy and
awesome is His name.

—Psalm 111:7–9 NIV

I do not take after my mother.

My mother's house, at any given moment, is spotless. Bedroom
cleanliness was not my strong suit growing up, and it was always a
tension point between my mom and me. She gave up on my room as
a teenager, but every other square foot of our home was pristine: spot-
free, dust-free, and clutter-free.

I would like to tell you, as a homeowner, I now possess my mom's
inclination toward cleanliness. In the interest of honesty, however, I
can't.

I would love to say I outgrew my messy tendencies like a child out-
grows thumb-sucking.

I didn't.

I wish I could offer you an "all-access" pass to my home, with full
permissive rights to pop in anytime.

I won't.

If one's home is a reflection of their mind, I am in big trouble. As I
type, the laundry my husband so graciously did five days ago sits folded in three separate laundry baskets. As hard as I try to will the clothes
to put themselves away, they stubbornly remain where they are.

Our game room looks like Toys "R" Us blew up. My nightstand hosts stack after stack of half-read books. My side of the closet is scattered and haphazard. My side of the bathroom counter is a brilliant hodgepodge of makeup, hairbrushes, and bobby pins. The floors need washing, the carpet needs vacuuming, and the shelves need dusting.

And then there are the fingerprints.

Evidence of my children's existence is proudly displayed on every glass and mirrored surface in the house. Attempts to wipe them away are fruitless. Before the smell of Windex fades, the glass is smudged all over again.

I get frustrated with the clutter, but the fingerprints make me smile.

When my son was four he left a full handprint on my car's rearview mirror. Every time I glanced up to reverse or change lanes, I thought of my son. Every image reflected in that glass was viewed through the print of his little hand.

One day, as Mike was driving my car, he looked over at me and said, "You really need to wash your mirror."

"Absolutely not," I shot back, "and if you wipe that handprint off, I will be so upset!"

I could hardly blame my husband for rolling his eyes. I admit I might have a *small* tendency to hoard everything my children have ever cut, colored, or created. But this was different. That small, pudgy handprint on my rearview mirror was symbolic for me.

What do you see when you look through the rearview mirror of your life? Failed relationships? Wayward children? Bad financial decisions? Missed opportunities? Some of our paths are littered with broken hearts and shattered dreams; some of us still haven't found our way back to the path. Some of us bear the marks of abuse or addiction; some of us have never managed to pull ourselves out of the mundane monotony of mediocrity.

God beckons you to look again, harder this time. Don't stare at the mistakes; focus on the Handprint covering them. Allow the backdrop of your life to fade to soft focus as the cross emerges through the pain. Don't let who you *were* define you. Let who you *are* glorify Him.

I am not proud of my messy house or my messy past. My heart breaks as I remember the anxiety-ridden young woman I used to be.

Nearly two decades lost in a haze of alcohol and bulimia. But I must also ask myself this: Would I have a ministry without my history? Would I have a message without my mess? Could I offer anyone hope if I had never walked through a season of complete and utter hopelessness?

I don't think I could. And because I know the hope I have in Christ, because I know the soft feel of grace poured out like rain, and because my failures spotlight His triumph, I wouldn't erase a single thing.

He is bigger than your troubles. His comfort is greater than your pain. His victory covers your failures.

The tragedy is never the sin-riddled life. Grace, mercy, and forgiveness are ours in Christ. Our old selves were crucified with Jesus so that sin would lose its power over us. The tragedy is failing to look at our lives through the Holy Handprint that covers it.

FINAL THOUGHTS

I remember my first Bible study like it was last week.

I was attending a giant Texas-sized megachurch in Grapevine, Texas, and after growing up in the quiet liturgy of our denomination, it was an assault of the senses in the best way.

Instead of a choir they had a rock band, instead of handouts we had video announcements. I didn't have to scramble to find the song in a hymnal, the words splashed across the giant screens as *American Idol*-caliber worship leaders encouraged us to clap our hands and sing along.

It was as if I'd died and gone to heaven.

After a few weeks I joined the church, signed up for a small group, and enrolled in a Bible study taught by Beth Moore.

On my first day, clutching my *Good News Bible* in one hand and my workbook in the other, I found the room and nervously walked in. I scanned my surroundings, trying to figure out which one was Beth Moore so I could introduce myself.

A pretty brunette passing out hugs and handshakes seemed to be at the center of things, so I approached her with a smile.

"You must be Beth," I said, sticking out my hand.

She looked at me, puzzled, and said, "Excuse me?"

"You're not Beth Moore?" I asked, feeling my cheeks begin to flush.

A smile flashed across her pleasant face. "Beth *Moore*?" she exclaimed, "Oh no, I'm not Beth. My name is Tianne. I'm the facilitator. Beth Moore is the teacher, but we'll be watching the lessons on video."

Then she gently asked, "Is this your first Bible study?"

"Yes, it is," I replied.

"Are you new to the church?"

"Pretty new," I admitted.

"Well," she said, guiding me by the elbow, "let's introduce you to some of the women. You are going to love this study!"

She was right.

As I watched the petite, passionate blond-haired Bible teacher, a fire ignited within me.

Beth Moore spoke of Jesus as though He was her best friend, as though she talked to Him every second of every day, and as though *He spoke back.* She called Him her Rock, her Rescuer, her Savior and Redeemer; an ever-present help in trouble.

I wanted what she had.

I had been reading the Bible for years, but now I started to devour it. When that study ended, I signed up for another, and then another, and then another.

What I discovered along the way is this: God does not show partiality to the Beth Moores and Billy Grahams. He does not save His biggest revelations for the pastors, preachers, and Bible teachers. On the contrary, God is always speaking. The question is, *are we listening?*

Psalm 25:14 says, "The Lord confides in those who fear Him; He makes His covenant known to them." Proverbs 3:32 confirms that God "takes the upright into His confidence."

Please don't miss that. Read it again if you need to.

The Lord, the Creator of the Universe, the author and possessor of all knowledge and understanding desires to confide in you.

In you.

He has things to say to you that are for your ears only, secrets He won't give to Beth Moore, Billy Graham, your pastor, or me, for that matter.

He is waiting on you.

I hope and pray that *Holy Hiking Boots* has inspired, encouraged, and comforted you. I pray that you see the beauty of the risen Christ pressed on each page, but please, do not let this book or any other ever replace time in the Scriptures.

Don't settle for my stories. Let the Lord write your own. The most precious times in my life have been by myself, in my study, Bible and journal open and pen in hand. God has revealed things to me, rejoiced with me, chastised me, prodded me toward repentance, and caught my tears while I've wept.

He has turned my life inside out and upside down, and I would not trade one single second of the adventure. But the adventure starts and ends with time in His Word.

Strap on your Holy Hiking Boots, my friend. Begin walking with God every day and see where the road leads.

It won't always be smooth, but you'll never walk alone and you'll *never* be bored.

God bless you!

Bibliography

Ashcroft, Mike and Rachel Olsen. *My One Word.* Grand Rapids: Zondervan, 2008.

Crouch, Andy. "The Return of Shame." *Christianity Today,* March 10, 2015. http://www.christianitytoday.com/ct/2015/march/andy-crouch-gospel-in-age-of-public-shame.html?utm_source=ctdirect-html&utm_medium=Newsletter&utm_term=11609528&utm_content=340686743&utm_campaign=2013.

Estes, Daniel J. *Handbook on the Wisdom Books and Psalms.* Grand Rapids: Baker Academic, 2005.

Goodreads. "A. W. Tozer Quotes." Accessed August 17, 2016. https://www.goodreads.com/author/quotes/1082290.A_W_Tozer.

Jones, Layla A. "Mo'ne Davis asks Bloomsburg to reinstate player who insulted her." *Philly.com,* March 23, 2015. Accessed March 24, 2015. http://www.philly.com/philly/blogs/trending/Mone-Davis-asks-Bloomsburg-to-reinstate-player-who-insulted-her.html.

Merritt, James. *How to Be a Winner and Influence Anybody: The Fruit of the Spirit as the Essence of Leadership.* USA: Xulon Press, 2008.

Paleologos, Mary. "A Sense of Wonder," *The Huffington Post,* September 18, 2014, updated October 18, 2014. Accessed March 14, 2017. http://www.huffingtonpost.com/mary-paleologos/a-sense-of-wonder_b_5686811.html.

Smith, Robert D. "The Deeper You Go the Calmer It Gets." *Therobertd.com.* April 29, 2014. Accessed February 19, 2016. http://www.therobertd.com/the-deeper-you-go-the-calmer-it-gets/#sthash.zbpO1LXP.dpuf.

Sproul, R.C., "Nakedness Equals Shame." *Ligonier Ministries,* January 9, 2015. Accessed March 10, 2017. http://www.ligonier.org/blog/nakedness-equals-shame/.

Stuart, D. K. *Exodus*, vol. 2. Nashville: Broadman & Holman Publishers, 2006.

Tchividjian, Tullian, "One Way Love." Colorado Springs: David C. Cook, 2013.

University of Kentucky. "Did You Know that Kentucky is the Home of the World's Longest Cave?" *Uky.edu*. Accessed January18, 2016. https://www.uky.edu/KGS/education/mammothcave.htm.

University of Notre Dame. "Walking through doorways causes forgetting, research shows." Press release, November 18, 2011. *EurekAlert*. Accessed June 7, 2016. http://www.eurekalert.org/pub_releases/2011-11/uond-wtd111811.php.